In the Eye of the Storm

A Celebration of Family and the Real Purpose of Home

In the Eye of the Storm

A Celebration of Family and the Real Purpose of Home

by

Bonnie W. McDaniel

agl press

Manufactured in the United States of America
First printing April 1999

Library of Congress Catalog Card Number 98-73981
ISBN 0-9671858-9-0

Photo Credits:
Michael Spilotro (pages vii,3,4,7,11,14,18,20,26,30,31,36,53,
54,72,74,77,80,83,84,86,87,88,94,96,102, back cover and flap)
Adobe Image Library (pages 8,17,23,28,35,52,58,61,64)
G. Hampson, Editor

Front cover and inside illustrations by Erin Beth Harris
Book design by Spot Color, Inc.
www.spotcolor.com

In loving memory of my grandma, Lula Duncan, to whom
I will always be grateful for loving me and teaching me WHY.

Acknowledgements

To my husband and our children, thanks for being my family. To my special mother, "Sweetie" (Eula Lonon), thanks for knowing what I needed and how to give it.

Thanks to my literary agent, Barbara Lowenstein, who encouraged me to pursue my dream to become a writer.

Thanks also to Erin Beth Harris and Jennifer Sterling, the creative minds behind this book. To Sheri Gessert, for her assistance in the production of the book and to my make-up artist, Anita Henry thank you. To the eyes behind the camera, Michael Spilotro, there are no words, but thanks will have to suffice.

To my publicist, Michelle Feder, for your dedication and incredible insight, thank you.

And for the corporate supporters, Merrifield Garden Center, Eddie Bauer, Calico Corners, Laura Ashley, Heather Hill Gardens, and Total Crafts; thanks.

To the families who opened their hearts and their homes and assisted in this effort; Brian and Cynthia Cute, Bill and Karen Stevenson, Emmet and Pat Anderson, Claudia Lewis, Gordon Riggle and Jon and Denee McKnight, a very special thanks.

To Jim and Sheryl Canady, and of course Tony Brown, thanks for a great start. To Marcia McAllister, the editor for my newspaper column, thanks for allowing the voice of family be heard. To my six-grade teacher and friend, Erma Rush, thank you. To my advisor and friend, Conrad Hipkins, thank you! And for the spiritual advisors John M. Little and Marshall Ausberry, words will never be enough - for your prayers and encouragement, thanks.

To my special sister and best friend Harriet McMillan, you are a jewel! And to the friends and family who have laughed and cried with me throughout this process, but most of all for praying for me, thank you.

To the families I have known over the years and for those I have yet to meet.........

And last but not least, to my creator, for letting me be, thank you!

Deigratia,

Bonnie W. McDaniel
Spring 1999

Table of Contents

Introduction

They say that if you travel to the eye of a storm, at its very center you will find peace and calm. For my family and for many others, this is a place called home — a safe haven, and a place of peace, hope, nourishment, and growth.

It's hard to imagine in a world driven by e-mail and microwaves that something so simple and basic could be so powerful. We often hear comments like "things were different when I was a child." Yet, in an important sense, they were not. The basic needs of human beings for purpose, structure and consistency have always remained the same. And what's more, the methods needed to build strong family units are also the same. What has changed is our approach to family: parents today have more competing demands than ever before while also being bombarded with more advice than ever before. Meanwhile, our children are caught in the middle and being encouraged by society to "grow up" faster than ever before.

In the Eye of the Storm is a lantern in the fog — a book about simplicity, about what should really be important for children and for families. The lessons and skills taught to me by my grandmother form the foundation for this book. These lessons and skills focus on the importance of teaching and nurturing, while incorporating how-to's for important living skills like cooking, sewing, family entertaining, gardening, canning, and decorating. They redefine the contemporary ideas of "living" and "home" to focus more on nurturing and providing purpose for contemporary families. At the same time, they recognize our natural desire to exist in an environment of comfort, simple elegance, and style. These lessons focus on children, illustrating how to teach a child to plant a garden while at the same time instilling valuable lessons like nurturing, patience, planning and responsibility. They show how every act of living can be used as an opportunity to teach children and remind families of the intrinsic value of home. In short, my grandmother's lessons teach us how to use daily acts of living to fulfill our basic needs while building a renewed sense of hope, encouragement and purpose for families.

In addition to recounting my grandmother's basic common sense and wisdom, this book also tries to teach through example. In each section, real-life experiences are shared, with a focus on how to help children and families survive and grow through the good times and the bad. These experiences also illustrate how families can take advantage of special occasions like weddings, births, birthdays, and even death, to teach children how to live.

Finally, this is a book about nurturing and celebrating family and the real purpose of home. It shows how to pay attention to the messages communicated to us by our children, how to build a beautiful and nurturing home, and how to fulfill the basic desire of children to learn, work and progress. If we address the basics, starting with our children and families, then our homes (and perhaps even ultimately our society) will live, grow, and flourish.

Celebrate the home, and celebrate life! Discover the joy of good living, *In the Eye of the Storm*.

They say that if you travel to the eye of a storm, at it's very center you will find peace and calm…

Beginnings

Today begins the first day of the rest of your life. The choices you make today for how you live your life will define the future for your family — your children, your grandchildren and for generations of children to come. It doesn't matter where or how you began. What's important is where you are going!

Webster's defines family as "a group of individuals living under one roof and usually under one head." It further defines a family as "a group of people united by certain convictions or a common affiliation." Today's families can be best defined as a conglomeration of many different kinds of people from different backgrounds, all operating under the guise or appearance of a family. Missing from many of these families, however, is the bond or glue of conviction, and a common affiliation needed to hold them together.

I was not raised by my mother and father but by my grandparents, and for many years I did not fully appreciate how significant their roles were as substitute parents. Yet, in spite of the absence of my natural parents, the presence of my grandparents provided the necessary family structure and defined purpose — the bond and the glue — which helped set the tone for my life and the lives of my children. What I have come to understand over the years is the significance of that family unit and the things that were provided to me. A family serves two very important functions. First, it provides an umbrella of structure — that structure, of course, being the roles of the people who make up the family. Second, it provides a foundation of purpose for that structure. When these two important elements are realized, each family unit, including those that have been labeled as dysfunctional or unconventional, has within it the power to influence the future of our world.

I examined this idea more closely many years ago as I began promoting the message of home in my newspaper column and television segments. It's almost embarrassing to admit that like many others before me, I began by focusing on the important but superficial elements of homemaking such as the how-to's for cooking, sewing, gardening and decorating. Yet, the more I developed recipes and new craft and decorating ideas, the more I began to understand the important but missing element of this message. Certainly these things were important, but they were not what made a family run! These were all goods and services which could be purchased, so what was their real value or purpose for families (aside from saving money)? The answer, I concluded, was nurturing, and this can be provided exceptionally well through the commitment and structure of a family unit.

This "discovery" also led me to reflect on my earlier years and the constant "talking to" by my grandmother concerning why learning how to do certain things was important. I now understand, many years later, that her ultimate goal was to instill certain values and a sense of purpose which we all need to become parents and members of society. Although my grandmother spent countless hours teaching these important lessons, their effectiveness was realized only through the examples that were put in place for me to follow.

We all know the proverb which says that to everything there is a season, and a time to every purpose. One does not act independently of the other. For each act of living, there needs to be a purpose, both communicated verbally and defined by example. The time that is given each of us through the different seasons or stages of life are important to the process of teaching those lessons — each generation, in preparation for the one to follow.

Time is the opportunity that is appointed each of us, and by its very nature is something that must be taken advantage of while it exists. Once past, however, it is gone, and regaining the power of the moment is impossible.

How, then, can you begin the process of building a stronger home and family? How can you take advantage of the little things you do each day to help rebuild your family? Where do you start to build a foundation that will put your family in the category of "families most likely to succeed?"

You begin right where you are!

To everything there is a season, and a time to every purpose...

Starting the Process

There is a distinct difference between a house and a home. A house is defined as "living quarters for one or few families." In contrast, a home is defined as "a social unit formed by a family living together." In other words, one serves a physical purpose while the other provides for the spiritual and emotional needs of the people who dwell within that structure.

The purpose of a family's home is not limited to just providing food and shelter. It's purpose is also to nurture, and to provide basic training to our children for the roles they will someday assume in society. Each person who is born has a specific talent and a purpose which only he or she can fulfill. How well we nurture and prepare them will determine their success in being able to fulfill that purpose.

How can you build a home and a nurturing family? First, understand where your family is and who they are. Then, begin!

UNDERSTAND WHERE YOU ARE

One of the most difficult things to do is get started. This is sometimes due to our inability to recognize where we are. Getting started with the process of improving our home and family requires taking a cold, hard look at both and recognizing shortcomings and past mistakes — not an easy thing for most people to do. Though difficult, it is a worthwhile exercise because once completed, what will remain is a strong foundation upon which you can begin to build your family legacy.

If during the evaluation of your family you discover things that are difficult for you to accept, look at them for what they are, determine what you should do about it, do it, and then by all means move on.

The thought process in rebuilding a family is very much like that of rebuilding a house following devastation by a storm. A normal course of action is to first do an assessment of the damage, determine what worthwhile things are left, and then put together a plan to begin rebuilding. And like homes, the most well-built families are those that are built on firm foundations, so start here first!

UNDERSTAND WHO YOU ARE

Today's families are made up of any combination of people — from two-parent households to single parent households, from families where grandparents are taking care of grandchildren to families where two different sets of parents from previous marriages or families have come together to form a new family, or where older siblings have assumed the role of parent. Yet all of these families have something in common: they are families, and inasmuch, they all have their share of struggles.

Some families may have been convinced, though, that their situation is so unique and so dire that failure is their only option. Other families may have been convinced that their situation is so ideal that failure should never happen, and yet it does. Understand who you are — that your family unit may face more struggles than others because of its makeup or financial position, or fewer struggles, but that success is still up to you.

AND BEGIN

Learning how to live effectively in a family requires four important courses of action. First, choose to succeed, and choose this as a family. Second, develop a pattern of successful living. Third, surround yourself and your family with people who have learned how to live successfully. And fourth, when all of your physical efforts fail, remember there is love.

- **Choose to succeed.** Failure is a matter of acceptance. Changing your mind about who you think you are will change your future. You have the power to choose! This doesn't mean that succeeding comes from simply deciding to succeed, though: success is a struggle, and the very nature of struggling means that on occasion, you will fall. Falling, however, does not equal failure. What it does mean is that you have been provided with a new perspective with which to begin the process once again. Use those stumbling blocks and experiences as stepping stones to begin laying the foundation for what your family can and will become! And the key is to think and believe this as a family!

- **Develop a pattern of successful living.** The most important key to living successfully is that you match your thoughts and words with how you live! Your actions should become consistent with who you say you are! Becoming a successful family unit does not happen without a great deal of practice; the more you practice, the more successful your family will become. And, you must believe that you will become what you practice!

For example, if you determine that as a goal you wish to have your children receive a quality education, then you must begin the practice of taking an active part in their education. No one understands the goals you have set for your children better than you do. Leaving such an important function exclusively in the hands of a system outside of your family structure will almost certainly guarantee that your children will fail. Schools are the structure put in place by society to facilitate the transfer of formalized knowledge. Successful application of that knowledge is the responsibility and function of one's home and the people within it. By becoming an active participant in your children's education,

you will begin to practice what your children will ultimately become. Active participation by parents will also guarantee a more consistent application of the important values being taught at home.

- **Surround yourself and your family with people who have learned how to live successfully.** This concept is not based on economics or the location of one's neighborhood, but on the wisdom of other successful family units and the willingness to commit yourself to the cause of saving your family. Seek out and solicit the help of a family or families who are where you would like to be. Just as you learn to accept the idea of the impact of having your children live by your example, it is equally as important to recognize that you and your family can also be influenced by the examples of others around you. Breaking old habits will be next to impossible without a strong support system. A weak link in a chain cannot support another weak link. Attach yourself to a stronger link and after you have become strong, use the strength and learning experiences you have gained to reach back and support someone else. This is the key to building strong families, which in turn builds strong communities.

- **When all of your physical efforts fail, remember there is love.** A well-known passage from the Bible states that "love covers a multitude of sins" or errors. It is difficult at times to know whether you are doing the right things in how you are trying to raise your children. And to complicate matters further, the techniques that work for one child are often ineffective for another. If your efforts are steeped in a foundation of sincere love and genuine interest for the welfare of your children, though, the result will be children who grow into well-adjusted adults prepared to make positive contributions to society. Children are very forgiving and will usually allow for the errors we are bound to make as parents. Just remember to begin and end everything with love.

MORE PROCESSES

What does your family stand for? Do your kids know why they are important? Is your family enriched by the experience of rituals and traditions? Understanding and addressing these questions is key to laying the foundation for a strong family life.

Bonnie W. McDaniel

- **What does your family stand for?** A family that lives without guidelines or standards will eventually destroy itself and die. Each human being requires a set of standards or guidelines by which he or she will live. Those standards can either be high, or not high. Their quality or worth is determined by how well they are able to support and aid in the positive building of the family structure, which in turn plays a significant role in supporting and aiding our society.

As a child I remember listening in on a family meeting as some of the adults discussed the future care of my cousins whose mother had passed away. She had passed suddenly, leaving eleven children, and the dilemma was how these children were going to be cared for in her absence. I remember hearing my grandfather state that there was only one option available. His message was, "in our family we take care of our own." This declaration left no room for discussion and therefore everyone knew what was expected of them. There were no compromises! Without it having to be said, the women of the family knew that they were to step into the role of mother to guarantee that the "mothering" process did not end. They each understood that "welfare" and the state childcare system was not an option. This experience left an indelible mark on my way of thinking, and as a result I learned the importance of assuming responsibility and commitment to family.

As you begin to try to define the basic principles or convictions by which your family will live and govern itself, remember, this is the most important exercise you will go through. It is next to impossible to build a home without a blueprint. The guidelines or standards set by your family today will serve as a blueprint for the future of generations to come. It is also very important to remember that like successful designers or architects, much consideration should be given to proven elements used by those who came before. No matter how broken the pieces of your family unit, there exists in each of our pasts things of substance upon which we can begin to rebuild.

Make a list of what is critical to the functioning of your unique family. In defining this, remember, your family will serve to influence the kind of world in which your children will live. If our homes are in a healthy state, then our world will have no choice but to follow. Remember, the state of our world begins in each of our homes!

- **It is important that you are here!** Every child should be made to understand very early in their lives that their appearance on this planet was not through happenstance. He or she should grow up with a sense of their individual significance to their families and the world in which they live. As parents we should instill in our children the significance of who they are and the important role they must play in society regardless of what that role is. For example, if you recognize that your child was born to be a street sweeper, yet you had in mind when you first gave birth to him or her that they would be a famous world leader, as a parent you should encourage that child to the best street sweeper who ever lived. In recognizing their individual significance, a child will most likely grow up to be a person who is willing and able to accept responsibility for the role he or she is to assume. If a child does not understand and appreciate their significance, how then are they to feel responsible for the space they will occupy here on this earth?

In 1998, millions had an opportunity to watch the Oprah Winfrey show as she celebrated her birthday. As she blew out the candles on her birthday cake, she said something that continues to cause a sadness each time I reflect on her words. Oprah said that because she was a celebrity, millions of people were taking time to wish her a happy birthday, but there were thousands of others born on that day whose day of their birth was no longer something of importance. Oprah went on to say that because people thought it important to remember the day she was born, she felt extremely blessed, and she then took the time to wish a happy birthday to those people who had been forgotten. Even to this day I continue to reflect on her words about those forgotten people. Just imagine, the day of your birth passing uneventfully, each year, with no one stopping for a moment to acknowledge the significance of your being here.

Developing a sense of self-worth begins with subtle and powerful messages such as these. The most effective way to help a person develop a sense of who he or she is, is to first acknowledge and communicate the importance of that person being here. Commemorating someone's birthday is just one of many ways you can communicate to a person their significance. Acknowledgment not only teaches them to value their own life, it teaches them to value the lives of others. It is very difficult for a person to love and value the lives of others if they have not been taught to first value and love their self. The first step in learning how to love oneself is to be loved, and this process should begin at home. Sensitizing our children to the importance of life begins with a small yet powerful message such as this.

Just as it is important to celebrate your children's birthdays, it is equally as important to teach them to do likewise for the important people in their lives. It doesn't have to be an elaborate expression and they should be encouraged to make the process of giving something that requires a certain amount of thought as well as something that will give a part of themselves. This will also provide you with an opportunity to teach them the importance of giving of their time. By doing this you will de-emphasize the value of material things and help to develop a true sense of the deeper meaning of giving and caring in dealing with those around us.

Homemade greeting cards or personal notes are wonderful expressions to share with others. And for children, there are added benefits of improving their writing skills, developing their creative talents and experiencing the real joy of giving. Understanding the joy in giving is one of the secrets to developing one's own personal happiness.

- **Developing family traditions and the importance of rituals.**
Traditions and rituals are important to families because it is through these that we gain a sense of our individual significance and our purpose within the family unit. Most of us grew up taking part in things like family reunions, Christmas, or other established holidays and traditions. These special times have been successfully passed down through generations, in spite of the demise of the traditional family structure. It is through tradition that we also discover the value of our own individual significance. A family which does not practice traditions will most likely be a family without strong bonds or ties to one another.

Late spring and early summer is the time of year when I begin to prepare for the holidays. Like my grandmother before me, I have continued with the ritual of planning well in advance for the things that will come. Each year as we plan our garden and begin to partake in the bounty of the gardens of others at our local farmer's market, my daughter and I contemplate what to plant or "put-away" as gifts for friends and family.

In addition to this annual making of fruit butters, potpourri and dried flowers in the Spring and Summer months, my daughter and I also have an annual scavenger hunt in the Fall. During our hunt we look for unusual vines, nuts and other items suitable to include on gift packaging, decorative wall hangings or as a part of a gift itself.

A couple of years ago, I badly sprained my ankle, which meant that my daughter and I might miss our scavenger hunt. Luckily, our hunt ended up being postponed for only a month. During our walk my daughter commented how much she looked forward to this special time together and how disappointed she would have been had we not been able to keep up our annual ritual. Our basket was quickly filled with plenty of interesting finds that year, but I think the greatest find was the wonderful gift of time given to both of us to add yet another memory to the pages of the book that make up my daughter's life.

It is also through tradition that we are able to define the purpose for those things set aside to honor the existence of one's family. An individual who grows up in a family without strong bonds or ties will also find it difficult to commit himself or herself to things involving people and things outside of his or her home. This is an important consideration as successful communities are nothing more than groups of committed individuals from different families with different backgrounds who live and work together toward a common goal.

How, then, does a family which is without defined traditions begin to establish purpose and value in the things they do on a daily basis? You begin with what you have, right where you are!

It is important to first understand that establishing tradition does not require an act of grandiosity. In other words look for and embrace the simple things in life. A tradition is anything you choose to do with your family that has been set apart to be done at a specific time on a consistent basis. Simple things requiring minimal fuss and maximum experience are the most effective.

One good example of a family tradition with a far-reaching impact is exemplified in the family of a good friend of mine whose tradition is going to brunch each Sunday following worship service. What is significant about this is not so much the brunch itself, but the coming together of family members on a consistent basis at a specific time. This is time that is adhered to and looked forward to by each member of her family as an opportunity to share in the special things that are taking place in each of their individual lives. What also makes this time especially significant is that as four generations from different households of this family come together each week, they are impressing upon the minds of the younger children the value and importance of their family. More importantly however, is that these children are gaining an understanding of the importance of their individual existence within that family unit.

In my own family, some of our rituals include Sunday afternoon walks, a trip to the local ice-cream parlor on Friday night, a special lunch to end and begin each school year, apple picking in the fall of each year, plus a list of other small things that have become significant in each of our lives. As a young lady, I recall Saturday afternoon was designated as the time I would usually try out a new cake recipe as dessert for Sunday dinner. My mother and I spent countless hours together each Saturday afternoon as she began preparing Sunday dinner while I whipped up a new dessert. After becoming a wife and starting my own family, although I lived 1100 miles away, we continued to keep our date on Saturday afternoon discussing what was for dinner on Sunday, as we cooked together over the telephone. This ritual of making Sunday dessert on Saturday afternoon has now been assumed by my daughter, and so the tradition continues.

If you are having difficulty getting started, begin by re-examining some of the traditions practiced by your grandparents many years ago. Talk to older members of your family about some of their earlier practices or family traditions and consider adopting them once again. You will find that most older people enjoy sharing their past and will usually explain the significance or purpose of why these things were important to the functioning of your family at that time. Remember to have your children take part in this process. Take along a video or audio tape recorder and capture every moment. You may also want to look through old photographs to get ideas as a part of beginning this process.

As you look through old family photographs, it might also be a good idea to consider starting your own family memory book. A memory book is a great way to begin to understand the significance of your family's past traditions and help to establish the direction of your future. A suggestion would be to incorporate photographs from earlier generations and tie them into your present-day family memory book or album. Again, include the children in this process as it will help to establish in their minds the importance of who they are and the important role they each play in the functioning of your family.

Establishing Effective Communication

Communication is defined as "a process by which information is exchanged between individuals through a common system of symbols, signs, or behavior." For most of us, when we hear the word communication our minds immediately paint a picture of having to talk, or share what we know with another individual. Communicating effectively, however, requires not only the ability to effectively write or verbalize your thoughts, but the ability to listen, be consistent with your message, encourage trust, keep your promises, and avoid insults and harsh words.

LISTENING: YOUR MOST IMPORTANT WEAPON

Effective communication does not occur until you listen as well as speak. The very nature of parenting, though, sometimes encourages a mindset of counseling our children and trying to tell them everything we think we know. In many instances, this means that parents fall into the trap of talking incessantly rather than listening to what their children have to say.

For years I fell into this pattern of talking endlessly to my oldest child in order to try to impart the wonderful parenting skills I thought I had. One day after many years of going through this exercise, my son blurted out during one of our discussions, "Mom, you never listen to what I have to say." I was completely surprised by his comment, and I must admit

my ego was bruised a little, but from that moment on I began to understand that in order to communicate effectively with him, I needed to learn how to listen. What is interesting, too, is that by listening I was able to not only become a better parent, but it also allowed me to become someone who my children felt they could talk to. From the mouth of babes comes such wisdom!

Remember to take the time to have a conversation with your children on a regular basis. If at all possible, try taking long walks as a way to have a conversation without the usual distractions and interruptions typically found at home. If you are not able to get out for a walk, try turning off the ringer on the telephone and be sure to turn off the radio and the television.

Listening is perhaps one of the most effective tools each parent has available to them. It doesn't require money, a fancy house or an advanced degree in psychology. Fortunately, you can become a good listener without any of these things. By listening to your children you will learn what you need to know in order to be an effective parent because if you listen, they will tell you.

Our society places a great deal of confidence in psychologists when trying to understand the makeup of people and how to effectively deal and communicate with them. If, however, you have ever had the occasion to speak with a psychologist or observe the methods used to perform their services you will notice that what they do best is listen. I am not suggesting that the value of psychologists should be undermined, but that as a parent you have the ability to make a tremendous impact in the lives of your children simply by listening to what they have to say.

It is natural for parents to want to exercise their authority by telling their children what they want them to know. As difficult as it may seem, however, you should make every effort not to give in to the urge to speak. Instead, try to encourage dialogue by asking their opinion on different subjects which interest them, and then listen!

Bonnie W. McDaniel

BE CONSISTENT

Consistency is probably the biggest yardstick your kids will use to measure your communication skills. Many things contribute to the loss of trust but perhaps the most common is a parent's lack of consistency. It is extremely important that parents be consistent in dealing with their children. Many parents, myself included, have had occasions where because of guilt or being pressured by a child or a situation, we have allowed ourselves to waver in our message concerning discipline or commitments made to our children. Although at the moment, giving in to pressure or changing a rule may appear to be the best solution, in the long run it is better to allow the rules to stand. The fallout from standing firm will be temporary and will usually end the moment the situation is over, with no lingering feelings of doubt in the minds of your children questioning your consistency.

ENCOURAGE TRUST

Trust is the foundation upon which solid relationships are built. One of the biggest roadblocks in communicating between parents and children is the lack of trust. One common mistake made by parents which usually leads to this loss of trust is betraying a confidence that is shared with you by a child. If your children come to you in confidence to share a problem or a secret desire, then it is important that this discussion not be shared with anyone. Children need to feel they are able to trust a parent in all situations and with all things. A loss of trust can have far-reaching implications in the relationship between a parent and child and may also affect a child's confidence in him or herself. The ability of your children to trust you as a parent with every aspect of their lives is key in establishing and maintaining open and effective lines of communication.

Because of the nature of my work as a columnist, I must be very sensitive to my children concerning their privacy. During any given day there are likely to be a number of interesting experiences that could be shared with those who read my columns. If these experiences can provide value to families who might be going through similar situations, I am careful to first discuss them with my children and gain their permission before sharing that information outside of our home. If they ask that I not share the information, then it is kept within the confines of our home. It is tempting sometimes as they constantly provide good writing material, but it is more important that they continue to be able to trust me.

KEEP YOUR PROMISES

Don't make promises you can't keep! This is perhaps the toughest of all rules to follow because no one is able to predict the future. In situations where plans are being made too far into the future, it is best not to share them with your children until the outcome seems imminent. Breaking promises over and over again will teach your children not to trust you. It is especially difficult to be close to or trust someone who does not keep promises, regardless of the reason for the promise not being kept. Children are very interesting in that they will only remember the outcome of a situation but very little of the details as to why the promise was not kept.

AVOID INSULTS AND HARSH WORDS

"Sticks and stones may break my bones, but names will never hurt me!" Do you recall saying this to someone as a child, usually to an older child trying to make him or herself feel good at your expense?

Unfortunately, some adults communicate with their children in a similar fashion. Unlike situations on the playground, however, where you were more likely to put the incident behind you, hurtful words spoken by a parent tend to have an effect that is long-lasting and much more damaging to a child. Cursing or hitting a child out of frustration only results in bringing up an individual who will eventually become an angry adult who is out of control or whose spirit has been broken and is therefore unable to function around other people. And although the use of profanity will usually get most people's attention, it will do nothing to nurture and encourage a child to grow into a responsible and caring adult. If anything, it will do the exact opposite.

Parents who communicate with children using insults and harsh words usually fall into two categories: parents who were verbally and or physically abused as children themselves, or those who lack the skills to communicate effectively and therefore hurl insults out of desperation and ignorance. If you find yourself in a situation where you feel as if you might lose control, try counting to ten, or try singing a song (in your head) in order to allow yourself the time needed to come under control. A stern look also works if you feel the situation requires some action and it is not safe to speak at the moment. I remember my grandmother was able to speak volumes to me with a simple look during those times when I misbehaved, and she never had to utter a word.

"I never had to apologize for anything I didn't say," said Calvin Coolidge. Parenting is one of the most challenging roles there is in our society. The pressure of being a parent can at times overwhelm even the best of people, yet, you must consider the long-term effects of what you say and how you say it in all situations and at all times.

AND A FEW OTHER TIPS

Due to the complexity of raising children, parents are bound to violate at least one of these rules of what not to do. If you have fallen in any of these areas, it is important that you recognize that this does not make you a bad parent. The nature of parenting dictates that we continue to learn and grow each day, which means the process of learning never ends.

Here are a few tips for handling situations that require extra patience when trying to communicate with your children:

- **Remember, you are the adult and not the child.** Competing with your children for attention by trying to outscream them during tense moments will only give you a head-ache and make you hoarse. For the moment, remove your personal feelings from the situation and remember that a fire will not burn without fuel. Remaining calm and teaching a child, through your actions, how to vent their frustrations will usually cause him or her to realize the importance of being able to control him or herself. This is a lot more effective than trying to scream it into their heads. Be certain, however, to constantly make a distinction between who is the parent and who is the child as you want them to be clear in understanding that your calmness does not mean you are accepting of their bad behavior.

Nothing improves a bad attitude like a little hard work...

- **When children throw temper tantrums, they are usually lacking a better response.** Such a response is usually a direct correlation to their level of maturity and lack of experience in handling adverse situations. Most children will occasionally exhibit this type of behavior, so don't be alarmed and respond by giving in to the outburst and rewarding unacceptable behavior. Remember also not to add fuel to the fire by allowing yourself to lose control. Remain calm and let the child know that if he or she would like to get your attention, then it is necessary to communicate in a way in which you are willing to accept. And then explain what is the acceptable behavior.

- **If you can't think of anything good to say, say nothing at all.** In a fit of anger or frustration, it is common for most people to react. Sometimes the best response to a frustrating situation is to simply say nothing at all. By keeping silent, an amazing thing happens: you are forced to think. Thinking about a situation can give you the time you need to decide on the right response. Remember to talk with your child after you have given the situation enough time to calm down. It is important that he or she understands that calmness in handling a matter does not mean you are weak or accept the situation.

- **Nothing improves a bad attitude like a little hard work.** If you are dealing with teens, it can become quite frustrating when you realize their main goal at times is to be as difficult as possible. I remember an incident involving my husband and son, when it became obvious after several minutes of trying to gain his cooperation on a matter, that he was not going to cooperate and was determined to get his way. After stating to him several times that he needed to calm himself, my husband finally ordered him to clean up the back yard. What made this seem especially harsh at the time was that the yard was filled with freshly fallen autumn leaves and his order was that he was to remove them without using a leaf blower or a yard rake. He was instead to use his hands, which meant one leaf at a time. I must admit that I tried to interfere and convince my husband to rethink his request, but he refused to back down. I later discovered that he never expected him to clean the yard entirely by hand, but hoped it would give our son plenty of time to think about his actions as well as allow him the opportunity to regain his composure. His point was well-taken, as after about an hour or so our son apologized and was able to see my husband's point of view. In the end they both worked in the yard

Bonnie W. McDaniel

together raking and blowing leaves, completely forgetting the incident that had taken place earlier. More importantly, however, was the wonderful lesson learned by our son concerning self-control.

- **When you can't find the right words to say, write a letter.** Very often, the best way to get your message through to a child is to write it down. It is sometimes easier to communicate a point to a child through the written word simply because non-verbal communications such as body language very often gets in the way of the point you are trying to make. Writing also allows you to think about exactly what it is you wish to say without risking saying the wrong thing. A good rule of thumb to use is when you find yourself very angry or frustrated with your child, write down your thoughts immediately and put your letter aside until the next day or allow several hours to pass before giving it to them. If after a reasonable time period has passed you are satisfied that it is what you wish to say, then pass it on.

- **Time outs are for parents, too.** On occasion I have found myself at a complete loss in dealing with a difficult situation involving my children. In situations like this I usually order myself to take a time out. My time outs usually mean taking a long walk, weeding my garden or cleaning out a closet. It is interesting that no matter what the situation, it always looks differently an hour or two later, especially after a little positive physical exertion. I have also written letters as a method of venting my feelings and afterwards torn them up. The exercise of non-verbal venting can be very beneficial in helping get through a bad moment with no one being hurt by words which cannot be taken back later on. Another benefit is that you will teach your children how they are to respond to conflict or frustration by following your good example.

Long after the situation has passed, what you say will remain and will either build up or tear down all of the good things you are trying to do as a parent. You can not take it back once it has been said, nor will you be able to completely erase the scars once it has been done, so remember to choose your words and actions wisely!

Meals, Manners, and Faith

There is a wise old saying that says the family that prays together, stays together. This saying should perhaps be modified to state that the family that prays as well as eats or dines together, stays together. And throughout it all, good manners and respect for one another are essential ingredients.

FAMILY DINNER

The family dinner is one of the most under-utilized opportunities for getting to know one another and to teach family values. Ideally, families should share dinner together every evening, even though scheduling this is difficult due to demanding work schedules, commutes, and after-school activities. Still, families should make a concerted effort to sit down to dinner together each day.

It is important to remember that this time should be devoted to catching up on things that are going on in the lives of each family member. This time is valuable and should not be used to engage in other activities which can take away from the purpose of sharing a family meal.

Many families have cheated themselves by introducing distractions into the dining room or eating area such as televisions or radios. This time should be devoted exclusively to eating and sharing with one another the things that are going on in each of your lives. One word of caution: do not make the dinner hour a time to engage in subjects that are stressful or use this as an opportunity to chide your children, as you do not want dinner to turn into an interrogation session. Instead, use this time to listen to things your children may want to discuss as well as share the good things that might have gone on during your day. Serious subjects should be devoted to family meetings, which can also be established as a part of your weekly activities. Use this valuable time to bond as a family and to keep in touch with the many changes that are taking place in each of your lives.

In order to impress upon your family the importance of the family dinner, it is also a good idea to make each family member responsible for planning and preparing the meal. Younger children should be encouraged to set the table while older children should be given the responsibility of learning how to plan and help prepare the meals. If your children are given the opportunity to take part in the preparation, it will help them to appreciate the importance of the meal itself. This will also provide you with an opportunity to teach other valuable lessons such as planning, money management, nutrition, organization and completion of and following through on plans. These are all valuable lessons that can be applied in other important areas of their lives.

Finally, having a regularly scheduled family dinner helps a family maintain its focus on what is most important. As members of a family go about their daily activities, it is reassuring to be able to come together at the end of each day to help to reaffirm in the minds of each member those things that matter most. This time is important too, in that it provides the necessary balance needed at the end of the day, especially in the lives of children.

Along these same lines, dinnertime helps to establish order in what is in many instances a day filled with disorder. As much as many of us tend to long for days of leisure and structureless schedules, it is reassuring to be able to know with some certainty what to expect at different times. Children especially tend to feel more secure when there are certain things in their lives on which they can rely. Bringing the family together for dinner each day provides this order.

Bonnie W. McDaniel

Dinnertime also provides yet another opportunity to tell your family how much you love them. We have all heard the expression that "talk is cheap." Of the numerous innovations of modern technology, nothing has been invented yet to convey a message of love and concern for your family like spending time with them. Calling your children on the phone to say "I love you" is a nice gesture when you are occasionally delayed because of commitments at the office. A phone call should not be used however, as a substitute for your presence because after a while, saying "I love you" will lose its meaning. Like most people, they will determine how you feel about them not by what you say, but by what you do.

MANNERS

The practice of good manners is the process by which human beings acknowledge and accept the existence and importance of the basic rights and needs of other individuals. Once this acknowledgment is made, people are able to respond positively to one another, communication is heightened, and as if by some great miracle, good things begin to happen. Social courtesy has the same positive and powerful impact no matter where you live or what your background or economic status might be.

It is an important part of your duties as a parent to provide your children with the necessary skills in order to prepare them for the challenges of living and working with other people. This preparation begins with practicing and teaching your children good manners at home. There is common sense in teaching your children how to practice good manners: by teaching them the art of how to be gracious or mannerly, you will grant them the freedom to be able to move comfortably and successfully within any and all situations in dealing with other people. There are numerous cases where heated arguments could have been avoided and in some instances lives could have been saved with a simple act of courtesy. It doesn't cost anything, and the returns are immeasurable.

Manners come in many shapes and forms. Among the most important are learning to say "please" and "thank you." In spite of the power of these words, they seem to be used less and less frequently in our society. Think about your most recent visit to a retail establishment. Did the person who handled your purchase take a moment to say thank you? If you were

Take the time to say thank you to your children

fortunate to have had the person extend such a courtesy, you will perhaps remember how happy it made you feel to have shopped there. Then, take a moment to think back to your last experience when that courtesy was not extended. Your reaction was perhaps to want to take your business elsewhere. No one likes to be made to feel that they are unappreciated which is exactly what happens when rudeness prevails.

It is important to the successful functioning of business and society that people practice common courtesy in dealing with others. This begins with teaching your children courtesy at home by practicing it. For example, this can be easily accomplished with simple things like saying thank you to a child when he or she does something to make a contribution to other members of the family. Take the time to say thank you to your children. What you will discover is that they will not only learn how to be courteous but they will also become more cooperative and search for ways to have you say thank you. Receiving praise in the form of a simple thank you is just one of the things most human beings long for as an innate part of who we are. A child's self-esteem is just one of the resulting benefits gained by extending and teaching them how to be courteous.

In situations where courtesy has been an oversight, encourage your children to respond correctly by saying to them, in a kind tone of voice, "you are welcome." In many instances you will find that it will solicit an immediate "I'm sorry" along with a special effort to be courteous in the future.

It is important to impress upon children that in spite of what might seem to be popular practice, a lack of courtesy both received or given is not the way life was meant to be. When teaching your children to reject discourtesy in others, it is important to make certain that the oversight be pointed out by simply doing what they know to be the right thing. This technique will be successful in most instances. My grandmother was fond of the saying that "you can draw more flies with honey than with vinegar." Pointing out a fault of another person should never be done in the form of a demand; instead let your kindness and consideration be the teacher!

When we examine the concept of teaching our children how to live successfully, it is important that we do not underestimate the impact of little things and the importance of putting into practice what is taught as a part of their daily lives. Remember, the key to living a successful life begins in the simple things we teach them each and every day, at home.

- **Table manners.** Over the years, it seems our society has become less and less concerned with table manners, probably because fewer and fewer families sit down together at the dinner table. Having dinner together as a family does not mean pulling out the TV trays and turning on your favorite television show. The problem with doing this is that you will probably spend less time communicating with one another and more time watching television.

To teach good table manners, it is important to focus on simplicity. Begin by teaching your children how to set the table. By setting the table you are making the unspoken declaration that something special is about to take place.

Preparation for dinner will set the tone for the expected behavior once the family has been seated at the table, which will in turn make your role as teacher a lot easier. It is important to focus on creating an atmosphere that is comfortable and encouraging to having family members share with one another. As often as possible, try serving your meals "family style" which means to simply place all dishes to be served on the table thereby requiring each person to prepare his or her own plate. This allows your children to practice the art of sharing, teaches them how to pass food around the table, encourages as well as teaches them how to say please and thank-you, provides them with an opportunity to reflect on the important things that have been provided, and encourages dialogue with other family members.

It is easier to teach a child proper manners if you take time to explain the common sense reasons why certain rules are important. Telling them to do it because you said so will encourage disaster and eventually lead to resentment in the end. For example, asking a child not to speak with food in their mouth becomes clearer when you follow up with the fact that their chance of choking is increased when they speak with food in their mouth.

You can also explain that looking into the mouth of someone with food in it is not a very appetizing thing for the other person while they are trying to eat. Encourage them to behave in such a manner to be considerate of those around them.

Offer further encouragement by being careful to point out your children's positive behavior. Remember, children, and people in general, are encouraged by acts of praise.

Another side benefit — but an important one — of teaching your children good table manners at home is that you will prepare them to conduct themselves properly and comfortably in situations outside of home — from the school cafeteria to the corporate board room. The adult world is full of situations where, because of a lack of training at home, people have been put in situations that are embarrassing and which hampers their growth and lessens their ability to interact comfortably and successfully around others. Teaching your children good or proper table manners will arm them with one of the key ingredients to leading a successful life. Remember, a well-prepared child will most likely grow into a confident and well-adjusted adult.

Finally, table manners are important because they help convey respect and thanks for the privilege and blessing of having food, shelter, and family. Recognizing this at every meal helps drive home the point to kids (and adults!) that we should never take our comforts for granted, and that we should always have empathy for those who don't have food, home, or family. As important as the family meal is to developing table manners, it is also a valuable tool for helping our children become caring adults.

FAMILY DEVOTION

So much has happened over the years to impact the way families handle the issue of whether or not to worship. A generation of children is growing up without a basic understanding of or appreciation for their faith, whatever that faith might be. If a child is allowed to grow up believing that he or she is the center of the universe, and that the people in orbit around them are all there is, what happens when disappointment, frailty, or tragedy occur, either in their own lives or in the lives of others?

Bonnie W. McDaniel

As a parent, it is important to communicate to your children that spirituality matters. Families — children in particular — need to know that we will all eventually find balance when situations and circumstances are beyond our ability to understand or control. It is equally important that children are taught early in life that prayer, faith, humility and many other qualities which worship develops are the most important elements to our being able to maintain that balance.

It has been my experience that when a family institutes a standard of worship, it helps in establishing or setting the tone for the kind of value system that will be supported within your family unit. What this action also communicates is that there is a certain standard by which your family will live and that the commitment is a unified family effort. By beginning this process very early in a child's life, you begin to build a foundation and establish a pattern of living to support many of the issues concerning principles and values that will arise over the course of their lives. Remember also that it is easier and much more effective to live a lesson than to preach it — do not try to teach this important lesson by "preaching" to your children. They will understand its true meaning by watching how you live.

I recall reading a sign once which stated that a person who stands for nothing will fall for anything. By taking a stand and setting standards you are making a statement that this is the creed by which your family will live. Your children will have a clear understanding of what they stand for and the likelihood is that they will not easily fall into situations which could perhaps put their future existence in jeopardy. And, in the instances when they do fall, they will have a roadmap to lead them back to where they should be. Children who live without principles or standards are usually at a greater risk for becoming habitual offenders within the criminal justice system, and may be more likely to seek comfort in drugs and alcohol, or become members of gangs or easy targets for those people in our society who are waiting to take away the lifeblood of who they could possibly become.

In addition to taking part in formal worship, it is also important that you establish a time for family devotion within the home. This could be a scheduled time to read your family devotional together and explain why certain standards are important to the well-being of your family. This will provide you with an opportunity to teach the application of religious principles that have been taught in your formal place of worship. This can also be used as an opportunity to communicate where and how these principles are to be applied in your home and in their individual lives.

Finally, take the time to teach your children how to pray, and then spend some time pray-ing with them. By openly verbalizing your concerns and desires for your family and your community through prayer, you are helping to reinforce in the minds of your children your commitment to doing your part in helping to make their world a better place in which to live.

Here are a few tips to remember in establishing a pattern of worship within your family unit:

- **Take an active lead in showing rather than telling your children what you expect from them.** The real lesson is lost when a choice is made to "send" rather than attend worship service with them. By taking the time to worship with them, you will communicate your full support for what you say your family believes in. Children find it difficult to understand or accept a belief system that is void of consistent action on the part of a parent.

- **It is a parent's job to teach values and principles to their children, not to force them to accept them.** You can lead a horse to water but you can't make it drink. The same applies to teaching children. You will find however, that if you are consistent in teaching and the application of what you are teaching by how you live, the process of acceptance will naturally follow. Human nature dictates that people will eventually migrate to that which they know and are accustomed. The key is to teach and live the right things and the rest will take care of itself.

- **Your children are watching you.** This is the most critical area of teaching that must be uppermost in a parent's mind. Whether consciously or unconsciously children are watching to see if what they are being taught is just a bunch of hype. For example, if your family is being taught that hate is wrong on Sunday, then it is important to remember that it is wrong on every other day of the week as well, and there are no gray areas. The quickest way to make a child turn away from what you are trying to teach is to live in an inconsistent manner. In other words, practice what you teach.

- **Tell them the truth.** If a child is mature enough to ask a question, he or she is mature enough to receive an honest and truthful answer. What should vary is the context in which the truth is spoken. In other words, tell the truth but put it into words that fit their level of maturity and where they are at the time. Remember, in order to establish effective lines of communication, there must be an element of trust in a relationship; lying does not foster a trusting relationship.

- **Do not make a habit of judging your children.** Nothing discourages a child's efforts more than to feel that he or she is up for constant review. The most effective way to teach a lesson sometimes is to allow the lesson to teach itself. Very often we do not give our children enough credit for knowing the difference between right and wrong even after we have made a concerted effort to teach them. Allow the lessons that have been taught to reveal themselves to your children through their own personal experiences, which very often might mean having them make and learn from their own mistakes. Remember, once we have done our as job as teachers, our function is to be there as support only. Allowing a child to live and grow through their own experiences will cause the lessons to take on a personal meaning for their individual lives.

- **A good teacher knows his or her subject matter and plans ahead.** The very nature of children dictates that they are filled with questions. It is important, especially on the subject of spiritual matters, that you take the time to study what it is you say your family believes and be prepared to answer questions when they are presented to you. You cannot teach something if you are unfamiliar with the subject matter. Something as important as providing a spiritual foundation for your children deserves your best effort and should therefore be given the proper study time in order to be prepared for the questions that will ultimately come.

Seasons

Life at home goes through many seasons — from the formative years (the time to build foundations), to exploration and discovery, testing (adolescence), young adulthood, learning to fly, going away to college, and moving away from home, both figuratively and literally.

THE FORMATIVE YEARS

The period between birth and five years old is one of the most critical times in a child's life. Many life-shaping events happen to children during the first five years. This is perhaps due to the helplessness, vulnerability and dependency a child has on those who are put in charge of caring and providing for them.

Building a foundation for a child begins the day they are born and continues through about the age of five years old. During this time, children are able to gain a sense of who they are and what is expected of them within the family unit. They learn how to communicate both verbally and physically in order to move about effectively within their environment. It is important to recognize that this time is critical in a child's life in establishing their sense of well-being. It is also important to understand that this is the time when they will gain self-confidence by learning how to first function

It is always a welcome moment when the Thanksgiving and Christmas holidays finally arrive. It is also a tremendous letdown once the decorations have been put away and the New Year's Eve celebration is but a distant memory. After so many weeks of endless activities and celebrations, many of us are left wondering what to do as an encore.

Each year, over a period of one week, we end one year and begin another with our own styles of celebration. And as we begin yet another year we contemplate what to do to top the year before. Many search aimlessly for another reason to celebrate. Of the 365 days of each year, we are reminded that there only 12 or so official holidays and when you throw in a birthday or two the rest are just days to work and look forward to the next official reason to celebrate.

Christmas Day of 1997 was especially quiet for my family as we decided against the usual full house of relatives and friends. We kept things pretty quiet and this allowed us to enjoy the company of one another. Although we missed the usual gathering of family and friends, the change was welcome.

Following Christmas dinner, we decided to accept an invitation from friends to visit them and their new baby. If there was a chance we had been missing the chatter and noise of a full house, our longing was quickly diminished as we entered their home. There were the usual toys covering every inch of floor space in their cozy home. In addition to the couple and their three children were grandparents and an uncle and his wife to be.

After spending some time visiting with the new baby we retired to the television room to watch a videotape. We were delayed in our efforts however, because their 18-month old had decided earlier in the day that the tape deck was a perfect place to stow away his toys. We were entertained while his father extracted each little toy from the VCR. I was especially impressed with the calmness displayed by the father as he went through the exercise of trying to render the equipment useful once again.

I commented to my husband later that evening that most men in a similar situation would have been on the ceiling, but this

father carefully removed each little car and plastic alphabet from the tape deck, smiling after each extraction. Meanwhile, the 18-month old watched curiously and proceeded to cheer with each success. When the process was complete the parents encouraged everyone present to cheer to celebrate a job well done.

In the midst of the waiting, the one year old became bored and wanted to move on to something else and decided that screaming was a good thing to do. Not the kind of scream to express displeasure, but the kind that said, listen everyone, I know how to scream. I was especially impressed with his mother and her response to this. Rather than try to discourage her little one from doing what is very natural for a one-year old to do, she managed to create a game where there were rules about screaming. She calmly called his name to "look" as she proceeded with a hand and arm gesture, very much like what you see an umpire do on a baseball field. At the right signal, they both let out a piercing scream. Once they were able to finally synchronize their screams, they both cheered for an accomplishment well done.

So often, we go through life missing such wonderful opportunities to celebrate the little things in our children and our families. We pressure ourselves to look for and expect the "grand" and very often miss the important little things which take place daily in each of our lives.

We forget that each day a child grows in any way is cause for celebration. It is through the celebration of small things that they learn to appreciate their value to their families, communities and the world at large.

It will be interesting to watch as my friend's little boy grows. Perhaps he will become a doctor or great world leader, or perhaps he will become just an everyday person to whom the world will pay very little attention. But, because of days like Christmas Day of 1997 when parents, family and friends cheered as he decided to express himself, somehow I know that the world will be a better place because he came to live here.

Bonnie W. McDaniel

successfully at home with family members in preparation for living and functioning later with other members in society.

How well your children respond to other people will be determined by what they are taught during this time and their ability to respond to those who make up their family unit. The ability to live harmoniously with others outside of the home will be determined by their experience of living in harmony with those around them at home.

It is also during this time that the identity of the child is defined within the family unit. After about the fifth year parents are able to pretty much determine the type of personality of the child and how they fit as individuals within the family structure.

During this time it is important to begin to teach children that the purpose of their family is to prepare them, through practice, for the roles they will assume later in life. It is important to recognize that people who are able to function successfully within their family unit will usually have an easier time functioning successfully in the world.

EXPLORATION AND DISCOVERY

The time between approximately five years old and right before puberty sets in is a wonderful period in a child's life. This is the time when discoveries are made using the basic foundation given during the building or formative years of a child's life.

Children begin to actively seek to form relationships with people outside of the family unit and are given their first opportunity to act on their own. The first friendships are usually formed during this time and it is also during this stage that they begin to understand how to function with people outside of the home.

This period is critical for parents to begin to establish a clear understanding of the kind of value system their children will follow. It is important to remain in constant communication as well as plan on teaching many kinds of activities in order to help to mold the lessons that have been taught during the formative years. It is also during this time that children begin to gain a better understanding of those lessons and how they fit into their individual lives. Parents should be very careful to be consistent in the things that are being taught during this time as it will help to further establish trust between your children and you which will ultimately help in matters of communication, especially in future years. An open line of communication is extremely important as you will not be able to know the effectiveness of your teaching without your child verbalizing their understanding of what is being taught.

Here are a few tips you may want to consider:

- **Plan outings or play dates as often as possible with children outside of your family nucleus.** By observing your child and how he or she interacts with other children, you will be able to determine how well they are learning the importance of things like cooperation, sharing and consideration for others. This time will also give you an opportunity to observe up close how he or she might be reacting to other siblings in similar situations at home, which is very often hard to recognize first-hand.

- **Play games of "what if" with your children.** This type of game is a wonderful way to gain a sense of the thought process your children go through when they are presented with different situations. This will also allow you to assist them with the thought process before the actual situation presents itself, as well as discuss why one kind of behavior is acceptable over another. You will find that it is easier to get children to listen to instruction if they understand why it is important. "What if" games are just one way a parent can help a child to prepare for what is likely to come.

- **Watch a movie or read a book together, and follow up with a discussion.** There are a number of fine examples of movies and books that carry wonderful messages that can assist a parent in instilling strong values in their children. Get in the habit of frequenting your local library and bookstore for ideas and suggestions. You will find that there are quite a large number that have not gained high visibility simply because they do not meet the "what's hot" criteria. As a side note, if you read a book or see a movie that you think has made your job a bit easier, it is worthwhile to take a moment to send a letter or an e-mail to the publisher to encourage them to increase their efforts

Good role models born in the home

Good role models are born and raised, not society-made. According to Webster, a role model is "a person whose behavior in a particular role is imitated by others."

One of the nice things about being a parent and spending time with children is that I have been able to gain a tremendous amount of insight into their pattern of thinking and how they view the world.

Over the years I have also observed one thing in particular that is consistent. No matter what you tell a child concerning how they should conduct themselves, ultimately, he or she will follow what they see you do.

A few years ago, I had the opportunity to observe a couple of two-year olds as they fought over a small toy. They pushed and tugged in an effort to gain control until finally, they began to hit and slap one another. The parent of one of the children immediately stepped in and began spanking and correcting her little boy by saying to him, "You are a bad boy."

Her son winced and appeared completely surprised by his mother's reaction. After hesitating for a few moments, he approached his little friend and, following his mother's example, slapped his hand and repeated, "You are a bad boy." At the time, we both thought it was pretty funny, but later, I thought about the implication of what had really happened. Little did this mother know, but she had assumed the position of becoming her son's role model.

Being a role model is not easy. There is a tremendous amount of pressure placed on an individual to always be on their best behavior. I imagine the reason many people reject the idea of becoming a role model is due to the pressure of having to act in a manner that is perhaps contrary to who they are or who people expect them to be. But the world keeps moving ahead and children continue to need examples of what they are expected to become. We have all heard the saying that a picture is worth a thousand words; so it is in the case of role models. A physical picture or demonstration seems to have a greater impact than just words when trying to present a model for proper behavior.

As a parent, it is sometimes difficult trying to figure out what to do to raise our children. I remember how terrified I was when my 23-year old was born. The one thing I recall asking myself over and over again, was now that I have this perfect little baby, what do I do with him? I recall thinking to myself, I am in serious trouble because I really don't have a clue.

Over the years, however, what I discovered was that in most instances, we really do have what it takes to raise our children. We simply need to trust our instincts and rely on the good things taught to us as children. And it helps to have good role models outside the home, and good schools, but these are not at the core. Role models who are appointed by society are in most instances not who we want our children to become. The problem with many of society's role models is that very often there is a standard applied that is based on things other than what is needed in order to become a decent human being. Good schools and extracurricular activities are fine and serve to make for well-educated and well-rounded children. What is also needed, though, are the small but very important lessons that should be taught to a child each day by showing and teaching them how to say things like "thank you and "please." These things will help to make a real difference in the world.

I have laughed about those little two-year old boys on numerous occasions, yet there is a part of me that continues to wonder whether or not the mother learned her lesson in parenting that day. There have also been moments when I wished I had had the courage to share with her once I thought about the implications of that experience, just in case she missed the point.

We can't always know what our children will become because as with most things in this life, there are no guarantees. But as parents and caregivers, we can make every effort to nurture, love, teach, and most important, set a good example in the best way we know how. And if we each do our part, one example at a time, we will all soon discover that the best role models are "home-made."

My daughter is fast approaching that age when the opposite sex is beginning to try to attract her attention.

A few months ago, a rather aggressive school mate decided to try his hand at flirtation and began a campaign to get her to notice him. Unfortunately, his idea had perhaps been influenced by some of the things he had seen on television or perhaps heard in some of the music he listens to. In an effort to attract her attention, he chose what he perceived to be the "cool" but hurtful approach.

I had noticed him throwing snow at her somewhat aggressively and had even spoken to him on one occasion not be so "rough" when playing with the girls. I continued to observe his different tactics as they waited for the school bus each day, but decided to try to let my daughter handle the situation on her own without my intervention.

The last straw came however, when my daughter came home from school one day in tears as a result of receiving verbal insults from this schoolmate. In spite of her protests, I decided that it was time to speak with his mother, who happens to be a single parent, about his behavior. And so, I took a deep breath and said a prayer before approaching her, as you never know how such an approach will be met in today's society.

His mother was a pleasant surprise, as she understood that I did not look at her son as "bad," but rather as misinformed. After explaining the situation to her she promised to speak with him about correcting his behavior.

What happened next completely surprised me as later that same day we received a visit from the mother and her son. She explained to him that I had something to discuss with him and he needed to listen.

My conversation, spoken as though he were my son, went something like this. "You know my daughter has watched her father and me over eleven years and what she had observed is that her father respects me and does not say mean things in an effort to get my attention or communicate a point. It seems you have taken a liking to my daughter and if you would like to get

her attention, you should probably try to follow the example of what she has seen demonstrated by her father. When it is time for her to seek a friend or companion, she will most likely look for someone who is kind in his speech and respectful to her as a person."

To this day his mother thanks me for the time I took to talk with her son. I have noticed that he, at least in the case of my daughter, has changed to meet the new standard.

As parents and caregivers, we can stop the madness which has become so pervasive in our society. We can regain the courage to say "no" when things are not acceptable and "yes" when they are. So often we look to the school system and our churches to raise our children. What we must remember is that our children should be raised by us. School, churches, neighbors, friends and extended family are there for extra support. The standard must begin, however, at home.

Bonnie W. McDaniel

on the behalf of families. Remember, it is always the squeaky wheel that gets the oil; let your voice be heard!

TESTING (ADOLESCENCE)

How well a child fares during adolescence is in direct correlation to the amount of time spent by parents to lay a strong foundation during the child's formative years. This is the time when all the lessons that were taught are put to the test through the challenges of things like peer pressure and having to begin the process of making decisions on their own. It is at this time, too, that you will be able to know the true worth of things that were taught in the earlier years.

Children who have been brought up in a nurturing environment will have a strong sense of who they are and will most likely find it easier to stand up to these pressures as well as be able to discern what situations are right for them without the constant intervention of a parent. It is important that if you observe your children considering the proper response to different situations that you allow him or her to act independently in their decision making. You should be there in the event you are needed; however, you should allow them to make their own decisions. You can be confident knowing that because you have provided them with a good foundation, they will usually make the right choice. Your role as a parent at this stage is to be there to offer support and encouragement but never as a controlling force in your child's life. With each new independent decision will come an increased ability for them to be able to stand on their own. Remember that independence is the goal, not necessarily success: the occasional falls or mistakes that result from independent thinking are very important, since this is when the greatest lessons will be learned.

Parents should also recognize that because of the complexity of the changes taking place, children will occasionally begin to experience feelings of loneliness and insecurity regarding who they are and how they fit in their environment. For those children who have been given the proper foundation, a simple reminder or occasional reinforcement will offer the proper support in order to get them through the uncertain times.

Consider the following:

- **Adolescence is the time for "dry-runs."** Depending on the level of maturity of your adolescent, you should begin to gradually extend more freedom to allow him or her to test and develop their decision-making skills. This is important since without practice, proper development will be virtually impossible as your adolescent becomes a young adult. You will also be able to determine how well they have been able to grasp the lessons you have taught up to this point by observing the choices they make.

- **Work to reinforce a relationship that is built on trust.** By letting a child know you trust them, you will encourage them to become more responsible. Take the time to explain the importance of maintaining a trustworthy relationship between the two of you. Make certain your children understand that a loss of trust as a result of their acting in an untrustworthy manner will impede your ability to extend privileges which are important to their development. And remember, too, that trust is a two-way street.

- **Have open discussions on a regular basis.** Keeping the lines of communication open between your child and you is the most important or critical aspect to navigating through the period of adolescence. A lack of discussion creates a lack of understanding. A word of caution: make certain to keep your discussions as light as possible because adolescents are in a period of their lives when most things are exaggerated, and they therefore tend to take everything to heart.

LETTING YOUR CHILDREN FLY

I remember vividly the day our oldest child, our son, discovered he could walk. He had spent several months holding on to furniture, to walls and to his father and me in an effort to try to put his little feet in motion. And like most toddlers, he took his share of tumbles as he tried to make steps for which his legs and coordination skills were not yet quite adept.

It was not an unusual evening. We had just finished having dinner and his father gave him a bath while I put away the last of the dinner dishes. A short time later we retired into our

There comes a time for all parents when it is apparent that the days of nurturing and hands-on teaching are over. That time is usually dreaded by most loving parents for it means a time of separation and change, but it must come just the same.

A few years ago I had the opportunity to share with my daughter the significance of that time as we were privileged to observe a mother bird as she diligently worked day after day to prepare a nest for her young.

Each morning we watched as she sat on her eggs and waited patiently for the new life that was about to emerge. We shared in her joy the morning we were greeted by the beautiful sounds of chirping little chicks as they beckoned for their mother to return to the nest with food. Each day we watched as she cared for and nurtured her little chicks until the day arrived when it was time to teach them to fly.

My daughter was heart-broken the morning we looked out the window towards the nest and discovered the chicks were no longer there. The cycle had been completed and the mother had set them free.

As parents and caregivers, this is one of the most difficult, yet most important things we must do in order to help our children reach their greatest potential. It is a challenge to know exactly when, as we, like our children, are also growing in the process. Unlike birds, however, each child is individual in their own right and therefore it takes astute and loving parents to know when the day of launching has arrived.

We are at that stage with our oldest child and have prayed and thought long and hard about his day of launching. There are some cases when the child will initiate breaking free. But in many instances, it is the parents who must finally say it is time.

This day of launching has been talked about between my son, his father and I for several months. There were certain plans with milestones put in place leading up to the day when he would finally be set free.

Unfortunately, our son is quite comfortable in the nest and remaining in the role of our "child," which is what he will continue to do as long as he remains in our home.

As parents, we have tried to be clear and understand what our roles as mother and father are supposed to be. We clearly understand that our role as parents is to teach, love, nurture and prepare our children for adulthood. It is our observation that we have accomplished that task to the best of our ability.

The time has arrived for our son to put his wings in flight. We understand that all the lessons we have tried to teach and the examples we have tried to live will gain clarity when we are no longer blocking his vision. He will realize his own strength when he is allowed to get up on his own when he falls; and he will, because getting up is what he has been taught to do.

We look forward to and will anxiously await the day when our son will come for a visit and introduce the strong man that is fighting so desperately to make his debut. This time of stress and fear will pass, and one day very soon, we will, as a family, look back and remember with much fondness the day our son learned how to fly.

living room, which was very sparse of furniture and perfect for a soon to be one-year old to test his walking ability without bumping into too many objects. I sat on one side of the room and my husband on the other as I began my usual routine of prodding him to "walk to daddy." This particular evening I released his hands from mine and without any hesitation, he began to move his feet in perfect one-year old stride until it dawned on him that he was doing it on his own. Our laughter and excitement served as further encouragement as very soon he began to run. We spent the remainder of the evening laughing and clapping our hands as he ran back and forth across the room becoming more confident with each new step and intricate turn . His confidence increased once he realized he was could walk on his own. What is interesting to note is that this realization could only happen through my willingness to let him go.

Raising children in today's society is especially unsettling primarily because of the high incidence of violence over which we as individuals have little or no control. As a result, many parents, myself included, live in constant fear of allowing our children the freedom to explore and move outside of the reach our protective arms. This was especially difficult for me in regards to letting go of our oldest child. In spite of what he was taught at home with regard to values and living in harmony with others, what did it all mean when he came into contact with others who were taught a different set of standards (or not taught any standards at all)? It wasn't that I did not trust my son, but I couldn't be sure I could trust those unknown faces of the people he was likely to meet. This point became even more poignant when American's favorite dad, Bill Cosby, lost his only son to violence. Here was someone who had done everything he could to provide everything possible to nurture and protect his children and yet, even he was not immune to what could happen.

In spite of our fear and concern for our children, however, it is important to allow them the freedom to grow into what they were created to be. There is no magic solution to handling this type of concern as what works in one situation can prove to be disastrous in another. So many things come into play when trying to determine just when and how a parent should respond in granting freedom to their children. The best advice across all periods of your child's life is to always keep the lines of communication open, and to help and encourage other families to take responsibility for raising their children. Every child who is given care and a solid foundation at home is one more who will contribute to society, and one less who will do nothing or even take away from the lives of others.

GOING AWAY TO COLLEGE

Maturity arrives at a different time for every young adult. On average, however, most college-bound young adults seem to begin this process of breaking free around the age of eighteen. One of the greatest unseen benefits of college is that it allows a gradual separation of the child and parent during a period when they can test many of the lessons that have been taught in earlier years. College also provides the perfect opportunity for your child to be able to test their interpretation of those lessons within somewhat of a controlled and protected environment.

During this time a young person is given the opportunity to gain a new perspective on how different things that have been taught should be applied to them and the significance of those lessons to the lives they hope to lead.

In order to provide continued reinforcement of things taught during the earlier years, parents should make a special effort to remain in communication through writing and periodic phone calls. Our age of technology has also provided a new and wonderful avenue for maintaining communication with students away at college — e-mail. This will allow you to keep in contact in a relatively inexpensive way with your child to keep them up to date on the things going on at home. If your home is without a computer or if you do not have Internet access, your local library can provide you with what you will need. You can use their computer Internet access to register and to communicate via the Internet with your college student. I have a friend who sends daily messages to her daughter who is attending college a few states away from her home. She is able to provide support as well as offer advice on the different things taking place in her new life away from her family.

Visits to your child's school, though — unless absolutely necessary — should be by invitation only. If you respect your child, allow them to determine when they would like to have you visit. You may find that you receive more invitations than you hoped for!

- **Care packages.** While in college, I always looked forward to Sunday evening, as did most of the girls in my dormitory. This was the time when a friend, who made a weekly trip to our hometown, would make his weekly delivery from my mother of food and other things she thought I needed. Although I was on my own, it meant a great deal to me to receive her wonderful care packages. Her weekly gift not only gave me something to look forward to, but it also helped me stay connected to my family and remember the importance of what I had back home. This weekly reminder also helped, in its own way, serve as a reminder of the important lessons taught to me over the years.

- **Books or articles of inspiration and devotional readings.** College life is typically spent reading textbooks and reference material required for a particular course of study. Books and other reading material on personal growth and inspiration are also very helpful in maintaining a healthy balance, especially once a young person heads off to college. It is important to maintain continued emotional development, and reinforcement, clarification, and inspiration in the form of reading materials can help with this process.

- **Local newspapers highlighting the positive things taking place at home.** Consider giving a subscription of your local newspaper to your college student as a birthday or holiday gift. This will help them keep connected, and also remind them of what is really important, especially during those times of loneliness.

- **Photos.** Start a memory book together before they head off to college, and send pictures of important events taking place at home while they are away. Also encourage your children to take pictures to add to their memory book of special events at college and to share these with the family during their breaks from school. This will allow them to keep connected to the family unit, which is extremely important for helping them feel secure during this continued growth process.

- **Bulletins, letters and programs from your place of worship.** As a project, encourage the younger children in the youth group at your place of worship to become pen pals with students who are away at college. This will accomplish three things: it will improve the writing skills of the younger child, it will give this child someone to look up to, and it will help your college student be accountable to someone while he or she is away at school. The accountability factor works with both the younger child and the college student. This will also help children who are in grade school better visualize their goals by observing someone close to them work to accomplish something that is perhaps their goal as well.

MOVING AWAY FROM HOME

As difficult as the process might be, it is important that at the appropriate time parents gently push their children out of the nest. This is important to allow the process of building a separate foundation for their adult life to begin. I have also observed that the longer the young adult remains at home the more difficult it will become for them to begin the process of accepting responsibility for their own lives. Parents should trust the years of preparation that have gone into helping their children reach this important stage. On the other hand, a parent who has not given the proper guidance and prepared their children will find this process somewhat arduous and will be constantly concerned whether or not they will be able to function on their own. Remember, if you have provided a good foundation you can be certain that even if your children stray from the course, they will ultimately come back to what they know.

Use this opportunity to work with your child to set up his or her new apartment. Consult with him or her to offer your assistance by donating items in order to help them get them off to a good start. If needed, you may also offer your assistance in areas like decorating, but remember, this is their new home and should reflect their own tastes regardless of whether or not you agree with their choices. Your role is to be there for support only! If they require your input, allow them to ask for it.

Parents who have provided the proper foundation are better able to enjoy this special time with their children and grow with them in their new role as a young adult.

Here are a few tips for helping your young adult prepare to move out on his or her own:

- **Set a date for moving out.** This date should be at least six months to a year away in order to allow enough time to implement whatever plans you might need to put into place. The important thing to remember is to be sure to set goals that are realistic and are flexible.

- **Establish a budget and amount needed to getting set up and define a plan for saving to meet that goal.** The budget will depend upon a number of factors including income level, possible contributions being made by family members, plans for living arrangements, and whether or not these plans will include a roommate.

- **Discuss contingency plans for handling things like alternate modes of transportation for getting to work.** This is an important consideration, especially if mass transit is not an option. Emergency car repair bills can quickly wreak havoc on a budget or jeopardize employment if emergency plans are not put into place for an alternate mode of transportation in order for them to be able to get to work.

- **Discuss safety issues and how to handle situations in case of an emergency.** Although this may seem a bit sexist, the reality is that this is especially a concern for females moving out on their own. It is always better to be safe than sorry, so plan ahead for the unexpected.

- **If moving out involves taking on a roommate, discuss things to be considered such as what to do if the roommate does not live up to the agreement.** For example, what plans are in place if a roommate does not pay his or her portion of the rent (at least three months should be put away in savings to allow for unexpected emergencies). Help define house rules that each person can live with and what to do if those rules are not adhered to.

Bonnie W. McDaniel

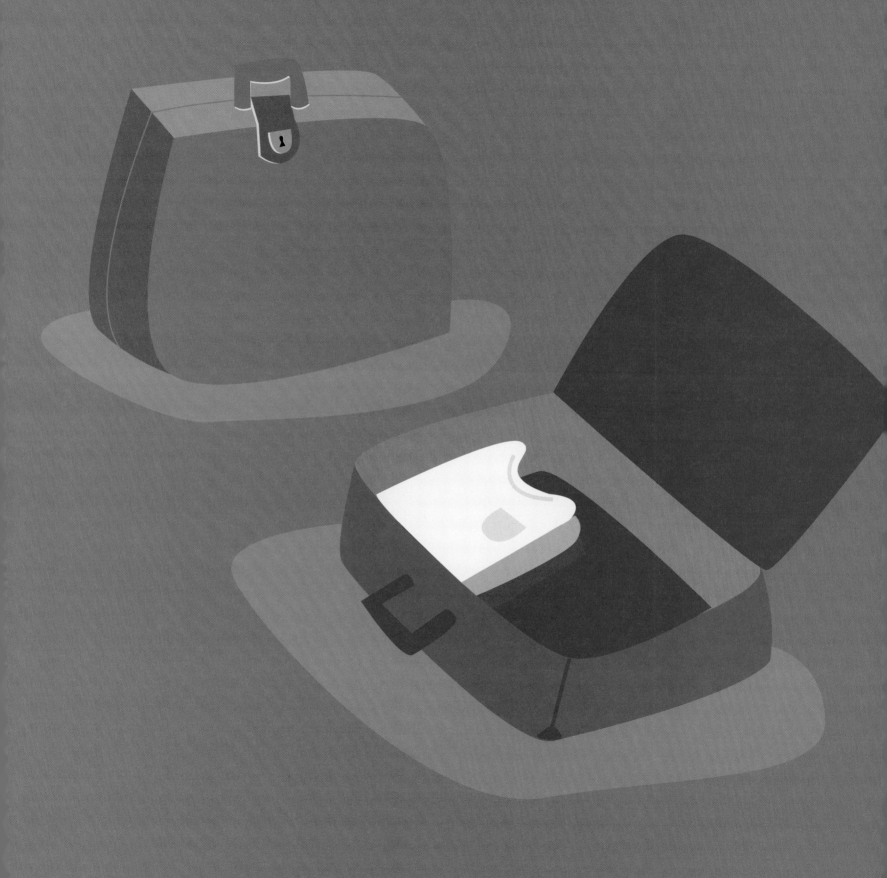

Time

Time is the most important gift and the most effective element available to a family in establishing a pattern of successful living. If you wish to impress upon your children their importance to you, you must show them through the time you spend teaching and preparing them for life. Loving a person means providing not only for their physical but their emotional needs as well. Saying "I love you" means nothing if you fail to make a commitment of your time in support of those needs.

Over the past few decades, most working mothers and fathers have been told that spending quality time with their family is an acceptable alternative to spending a large quantity of time. This notion is flawed, though, simply because the needs of human beings are complex and unpredictable and cannot be compressed into a predetermined schedule. Spending a few hours of "quality" time with your children on Saturday mornings cannot offer the same benefits as spending perhaps an hour each day discovering what is going on in their lives. Too much can happen over the course of seven days, much of which cannot wait to be given the proper attention.

Still, assigning quality time to fulfill physical needs makes sense — providing special help with a school project, for instance. It's the child's emotional needs which are not easily assignable to a set calendar or schedule. It is hard to determine when a child will need the support of a loving and caring parent to guide them through a difficult situation. Spending more time with your children, then — quality or otherwise — will increase the possibility of your being there at the time you are most needed. Raising children requires being available at any moment on a consistent basis in order to teach and guide them through the difficult maze of growing up. It is not possible to put a child's emotional needs on hold; it is something that must be dealt with as each situation presents itself.

So how, in practical terms, can families spend more time together? Some of the ideas covered earlier in this book are helpful — having dinner together every night, as a family, attending worship services together, performing family traditions together, and more. For many families who are in situations where both parents must work, evenings and weekends are all that is left, and this time should be centered around their children. Many parents balk at this reality and ask, "What about our needs?" The reality, though, is that when you decide to become a parent, your personal needs become second to the needs of your children. Children are not projects that can be put on hold until you find the free time to devote to them. The greatest dividends will be paid on those efforts that are made early and consistently in the lives of your children. You have the choice of investing early with a strong chance of a good return, or investing later when little or no return is almost guaranteed. The fact is that you will invest one way or the other. Perhaps a good sign for parents to post on the refrigerator as a constant reminder of the importance of investing in their children is "pay me now, or pay later."

Parents must also make the time to get involved with things that are important to their children outside the home. Become an active member of your children's school PTA and volunteer to spend some of your time on projects and at functions during the school day. This will make such a difference in the way your children conduct themselves as well as communicate to teachers that your child's education and well-being is important to your family. If you are having a difficult time trying to figure out how to find time during the day, why not approach your place of employment to suggest dividing your available vacation and personal leave time into hours which can then be used to do volunteer work at your child's school an hour at a time. If each parent donated a minimum of five hours per school

Bonnie W. McDaniel

year, think what a difference we could collectively make in the quality of our schools and in the lives of our children. There will in many instances be time that can also be given during evening school activities; the idea is to get involved.

It has been my observation that children usually become excited and take a greater interest in learning once a parent sets the tone by becoming involved. Your children will take great pride in having their mom and/or dad have a reputation among their peers and teachers for being a caring and concerned parent. Remember to also take time to attend programs or activities in which your children are involved. Many have had the unfortunate experience over the years of seeing children who search for parents in the audience who never show up and have seen the pain and disappointment of not having anyone from home to cheer them on or congratulate them on their accomplishments. It is clear that some children even con-sciously lessen their involvement over time in order to avoid the pain and embarrassment of not having a parent there. Programs for such occasions are usually planned with advance notice to facilitate scheduling. Once again, use a vacation day or personal leave time in order to be there for your children.

Before volunteering, analyze your strengths and talents and make yourself available in those areas where you feel you can make the greatest contribution. Remember, the strength and success of any youth group, whether at church, at school, or in the community, lies in inter-ested and dedicated parents. It is also important to remember that a church's youth group is there as a support only; under no circumstances should the overall responsibility of teaching your children be given over to anyone outside of your home. Analyzing what is being taught and who is teaching your children, as well as monitoring the quality of such programs is the ultimate responsibility of the parent.

There are numerous city and county sponsored recreational activities which are in constant need of parents to volunteer. Mothers and fathers can each play an active role in guarantee-ing the success of these programs by lending them time. Most fathers were at one time involved in their earlier years in activities like baseball, basketball, football or soccer. Now would be a good time to take a renewed interest in your favorite sport by becoming a coach or referee for your child's team. And if you are one of the non-athletic types you can always

The success and strength of a group lies in interested and dedicated parents

coach the computer club, or provide help with other things such as car-pooling, providing refreshments, making phone calls, printing up flyers, or any number of things needed to support such an effort. The key is to get involved!

FAMILY GOAL SETTING

Without a vision, people will perish! In order to know where you are going it is important to have a plan. In the business world, the saying goes that in order to be successful, it is important to plan your work and work your plan. It has been my experience that things that are planned and written down usually have a better chance of getting done. Begin now to set aside at the beginning or end of each year a time to plan with your family what you hope to accomplish in the coming year. It is also important that before you begin this process you take a look at what you have been able to accomplish in the year most recently past. As important as it is to know where you are going, it is equally as important to know where you have been. By looking back at the previous year you will be able to analyze those things that worked and those that didn't. This exercise will provide the perfect opportunity for you to learn and to teach your children how to learn from their mistakes and how to improve on your past efforts.

make a calendar...

One way to get started in putting together a plan for your family is to begin by purchasing or making a calendar as a family gift for whatever holiday your family celebrates near the end or beginning of each year. This calendar should be used to keep track of important dates for each family member and for things of importance to the family unit as a whole. It should be posted where everyone can see and use it. Be sure to write in important dates such as PTA meetings and school programs. Remember, develop the plan, then work it! This exercise will also benefit your children in many other areas of their lives such learning how to set goals, how to plan effectively, and how to work together with others as a team.

Also as a part of your calendar planning, be sure to include projects you may wish to accomplish around the house as a family. Mark your calendar to include things like times for planting the garden, times for visiting local "pick-your-own" farms to harvest fruits or vegetables, and more. Schedule time to teach a new skill (if you are not adept in crafts or

Bonnie W. McDaniel

the like, sign up for a class at your community recreation center), plan time away from home to vacation together (if money is tight, plan to visit a relative in the country or in the city with the idea that you will reciprocate by allowing them to visit your home as well), schedule day trips to attend free concerts or craft fairs, schedule time to participate as a family in a walk-a-thon to raise money for a worthy cause, or schedule time to do something nice for an elderly neighbor or a sick friend, or plan to visit a nursing home. Be sure to also check with local museums and the library to get a list of free or nominally-priced activities to attend during the year. In the process of taking part in all of these things you will be able to have your children begin to practice what is being taught at home while at the same time making lasting impressions on their personal development.

Responsibility and Accountability

One of the most important questions all families should ask themselves is "Why are we here?" There is much more to our being here than to "merely" have children, take jobs to support those children, and go about doing the things we do each day in the name of "living." Although these activities are all part being a parent, the responsibility of parenting goes much further than these activities alone.

My grandmother always reminded me whenever I left home to leave things better than how I found them. In other words, I had a purpose for visiting a particular place and part of that purpose was to not only learn from that experience, but to also leave a small part of myself behind. It is important that we teach our children this basic principle of living in order to help them to understand the responsibility we each have — to accept those things provided to us, but more importantly, to give something back. Giving back does not mean handing over of something physical necessarily, nor does it mean giving something grand. It could be as simple as returning a smile to a kind person who thought it important enough to give one to you. Going through one's life learning and acquiring becomes significant only when you take the time to teach and to give back what has been given to you. It is then that you begin to see the efforts in your life take root and make a real difference.

Consider the roles of runners in a relay race. To a runner who wants a successful race, a great deal of time is spent learning how to run and putting into practice those things taught in order to be able to run effectively. Running swiftly is important, as is grabbing the baton when it is passed to you, but what makes the race truly successful is whether the baton is passed to the next runner so they can receive it and pass it on to the next runner. Parents, guardians, teachers, neighbors and communities, all have the responsibility to pass along our time, knowledge and wisdom to each person with whom we come into contact. This is the key to making our world the kind of world in which we want our children to live. This concept works best, however, when it is taught at home first!

VOLUNTEER FIRST

Great mountains are moved when many hands willfully join together! Have you ever watched ants move things that are perhaps a hundred times their actual body weight? What is interesting is that they approach a task with the strategy of achieving through community or combined effort. They simply define the effort and call out the troops. Nature has so many examples of how to go about accomplishing things, we only need pay attention and follow them.

In a recent interview with the *Washington Post*, John Lewis, the silent civil rights activist of the 1960's and present-day Congressman from Atlanta, told of an experience he had as a child, which was the inspiration for his book, titled *Walking With the Wind.* "One day when he was four, playing with his cousins in the cotton country of rural Alabama, the sky turned black and began to roar and bolts of lightning crashed down to earth. His Aunt Seneva called the children—fifteen of them—into her rickety wooden home. They huddled there, trembling, as the screaming wind shook the walls and a hard rain battered the tin roof. And then the wind began to lift one corner of the old house. Aunt Seneva told the children to hold hands and walk into that corner. Terrified, they did as they were told and the corner sagged back to earth. But then the howling wind lifted another corner, so they marched into that one. And so it went. Fifteen children walking with the wind, holding that trembling house with the weight of their small bodies." Small hands joined together and summoned the power to hold back the forces of the mighty wind. Such power, such wisdom!

Bonnie W. McDaniel

To volunteer is "to enter into or offer one's service of your own free will." It is important to grasp the significance of willfully offering time and service so that you, your family, and your community can then appreciate the rewards of volunteering. Recognizing a need or a problem is important, but it is through the combined efforts of those who decide to do something that things such as the quality of homes begin to change and schools and communities once again become supportive in the proper raising of children. This is much more effective than the recent popular notion that the best way to handle our problems is to lock up or throw away those children who are perceived to be the cause for the pain.

Aside from helping build character and improving the lives of others and of the community, many parents may also appreciate that volunteering gives children something to do. This sounds a bit shallow — thinking of pursuing a selfless cause for selfish reasons. But the fact is that not every child can fill their day with their own schoolwork, chores, and creative pursuits, and by teaching your children the importance of volunteer work, and by taking part in this work with them, you get the best of both worlds — enriched lives and communities, and busy children. My grandmother was fond of the saying that "an idle mind is the devil's workshop." She believed that a busy child is a purposeful and industrious child. It is difficult for a child who is busy doing for others to find time to contemplate involving him or herself in things that are contrary to the positive building of their role in society. But even if you and your kids are already too busy to volunteer, you should make time anyway, for the selfless reasons. The rewards far outweigh the effort, and produce deep and lasting impressions on a child's maturity and accountability, and also help deepen the bond within families and communities.

Following are just a few examples of things you and your family can do as volunteers:

- **Nursing Homes.** One of the great tragedies of recent times is the putting away and forgetting of the emotional needs of our elderly. In many situations, because of the nature of physical and mental ailments, nursing homes are the only viable options for many families. What is tragic is not that our elderly are "put away," though, but the manner in which this is done. Human beings are not things to be disposed of simply because society has determined that they are no longer of any use. In putting away and forgetting about our elderly, we are also throwing away the valuable opportunity to pass down the vast wisdom our elderly possess to generations of children and adults. Children and the elderly have so much in common. There is an innocence and open-mindedness at both ends of the spectrum. Children are too young, in many instances, to have been greatly influenced by the experiences of life, and therefore their minds are open. Older people, on the other hand, have lived through many experiences and with it has come the wisdom which allows them to discard those experiences which sometimes cloud a younger person's judgment, and to come full circle to where they began. They are able to operate with an open mind full of hope, but with the wisdom of knowing how the story ends. Their wisdom is a wonderful jewel no child should be denied!

Contact your local nursing home and discuss with them their rules and guidelines for volunteering. You will find that most will welcome the interest and time given to making easier what is in all instances a very difficult job to perform. Some ideas may be to schedule time to play bingo or other favorite games of the person or persons you will be visiting. It is advisable to choose no more than one or two people to visit on a consistent basis in order to make the greatest impact. Initially, you may want to spend time with the person to get to know what their favorite hobbies might be and then have him or her share their knowledge with you and your child through either showing or telling you how to go about doing it. Reading is also a good way for your child to spend quiet time sharing their favorite story or interest or learning about the interests of the person with whom they are visiting.

If you prefer to go about serving the elderly in a different way, you can also assist your child in bringing fresh water to a resident, freshening up flowers that might have been sent by family members, escorting them on a walk, and more. Some nursing home patients or residents might also enjoy some of your child's art work from school which can be personalized and displayed in their room as a reminder that someone is constantly thinking of them. During the spring and summer months, a nice bouquet of flowers from your child's garden would be a real nice way to show you care. Check with the person in charge of volunteers for a list of other suggestions and remember there is always something you can do.

- **Libraries.** Most public libraries look for and welcome students during the summer months to work with small children in their summer reading programs. There is also story time in many libraries for your older children to participate in which can help to improve their speaking as well as reading skills while at the same time serving others in need. In addition to these activities, children are also given an opportunity to catalog and file books, assist in the signing out of books, participate in library tours, plus a host of other functions to assist in the proper running of a library during the very busy summer months. Volunteers allow summer programs to expand in spite of budget constraints, which in turn benefits the entire community. The age requirement will vary depending on your county and state, but usually children are able to begin volunteering in such an effort after reaching junior high school.

- **Hospitals.** Like most institutions that serve the needs of groups of people, volunteers for hospitals are always in great demand. Check with your local hospital to learn about the programs available for people wishing to volunteer their services.

  This is an activity that is best performed by high school students. Many hospitals have a "candy-striper" program for volunteers. Check with your area hospital for details on how you can get started.

  In many hospitals, there are also programs within the children's ward. Services such as reading books, playing games or simply entertaining some of the children is always something a young person can do to make a difference.

- **Schools.** Parent Teacher Associations and Organizations are always seeking the active participation of parents and children alike in order to support their needs. It is important that your children grow up in a home where their parents dedicate time and effort to the cause of their education.

  You will find that in many instances, the difference between a mediocre school and one that is superior in its effectiveness is the result of the involvement of parents and children in the educational process. Remember the analogy of the ants. I have throughout the years of my children being in school made certain to become active in the school's PTA/PTO program. By doing this I have been communicating two very important messages to them. First, they will automatically assume that this is how things are to be done when they become parents, and will not need someone else to tell them. Second, my involvement as a parent allows me to be able to define what is needed in order to help my children receive the greatest benefit through and from the educational process.

Through the PTA, some of the examples of projects completed by students and parent volunteers include:

- fundraising for computers or other needed equipment
- school beautification projects
- the "adoption" of elderly residents who can share their wisdom with the schools
- corporate partnerships which have aided in shadowing and mentoring programs for students as well as the donation of computer equipment for classrooms
- and many other programs too numerous to list!

The idea is that it only takes the willingness of concerned and dedicated parents setting the example for their children in order to make a difference in the quality of education. However, in order to make sure your children are receiving the best education available to them, it is important that both the child and parent be involved. Parents and children, working in concert with teachers and administrators, can make a difference in the quality of education received by each child in this country. And the more you involve yourself in raising standards and contributing to the quality of education being provided to your children, the more you will find people outside your school willing to also become involved. Remember that it all begins with your commitment to get involved.

- **Parks.** If your town doesn't currently have a "Spruce Up Your Park Day," perhaps you should suggest one at the next town hall meeting. Make a suggestion to help clean up a lake, pick up trash in the parks and around public buildings, and plant flowers and trees in the Spring — all great ways to teach your children how to give back to the community. You will also find that once a child has participated in cleaning or fixing up, it is not likely that they will be inclined to litter or take away from any of their efforts. This activity is something that should definitely have the participation of one or both parents. It is important to the process of teaching that you do so by example. This is also a great way to spend time with your children while at the same time working to benefit your community.

THE POWER OF MENTORING

Volunteering is a powerful force indeed. One type of volunteering not discussed above is mentoring. Very often we are reminded of the importance of passing along what we know to a needy child — perhaps one who is without the benefit of a mother or a father in order to serve as personal role models. This is an extremely worthwhile effort and has proven to be one of great value over the years. Your local place of worship or community center are good places to start if you are either looking for a mentor or thinking of becoming one.

Aside from one-on-one mentoring, also consider the tremendous possible benefits of families mentoring families. In an earlier chapter I mentioned the idea of seeking out and attaching your family to one which represents what you are trying to become. To those families who recognize the success of what they have managed to do within their family units, imagine the tremendous impact you can make in your community by passing along your knowledge and support to families who are struggling to keep themselves together.

Following are some suggestions for starting and managing a family mentoring group in your community:

- **Begin with your place of worship or local community center.** Many groups that are organized to provide spiritual guidance and community services are always looking for ideas and ways to strengthen and support their immediate community. Consider approaching either your place of worship or your local community center with the idea of starting or having them start a family mentoring group. You will find that in most instances your ideas will be well-received and that there are probably available resources to help you get started.

- **Remember, you are there to offer support and advice, not to assume control over the lives of the family you are mentoring.** If you are offering your services to have your family act as a mentor, remember to stay focused on exactly what role you will play in this process. Remember, that in order for your mentoring to be effective you must provide the necessary room to allow for your mentee family to stand on its own.

- **Encourage the mentee family to work out personal matters on their own.** Becoming personally involved in your mentee family affairs is something you should try to avoid at all costs. To do so will run the risk having your family become at odds with one another by taking sides on issues which you perhaps do not fully understand. Remember your role is to be there to offer support and guidance only.

- **Pass along any special skills you might have to help your mentee family.** If your family has the knowledge of how to do certain things, share that knowledge with another family. This will help to strengthen their family in areas that are perhaps needed in order to help them build a strong family unit. I have over the years shared my gardening knowledge with young mothers by encouraging them to plant gardens with their young children. In most of these cases, these mothers and children have gone on to become avid gardeners and it has helped to strengthen the relationship between parent and child.

HOLDING CHILDREN ACCOUNTABLE

As a parent, it is easy to understand the personal pride we wrap up in our children. For most of us, we are convinced that how well our children fare in life is a direct reflection of how well we have raised them. There are many situations where a child went astray because of what was taught (or not taught) at home, and the examples that were in place (or not in place) for that child. However, there are also many situations where everything was done the "right" way, yet in spite of the efforts of parents, things still didn't turn out the way they were expected. One thing is certain, though: teaching children to be accountable for their actions is a vital lesson to teach; whether or not your children learn that lesson is not always within your control.

Very often, parents — especially with the first child — will unwittingly prevent children from becoming accountable by protecting them from painful situations. It is often through these very situations, though, that children develop character. My grandmother and my adopted mother stated to me over and over through the course of my growing up, "what doesn't kill you will only make you better and stronger." Such wisdom, such power in those words. It is okay for children to experience pain and to fail. I am not advocating creating painful situations in order to teach your children valuable lessons about life. What I am advocating, however, is that once you have tried to teach a child how to live and they then decide to do it differently — especially when it involves a decision between right and wrong — the resulting pain from their actions is exactly what they should be allowed to go through. Sheltering a child by removing the pain in order to give them another chance, for most children, does nothing except send a message that they will not be held accountable for what they do in life.

Teaching this lesson can be especially hard for single parents. I have found in my own home that in situations involving my oldest child, having my husband step in during my times of weakness and insisting that our son be allowed to go through some pain was necessary in order to teach him to be accountable for his actions. Another very important point is that children are both very resilient and patient when it comes to wearing a parent down. Don't allow yourself to be made to feel guilty or to give in to make it easier for your children, especially when it is clear that their main objective is to "get over." It is important to have rules and to enforce them from day one. Do not prolong the inevitable, which is to allow your children to go through pain when they decide to go against the rules, as the lesson will only be tougher to teach later on. They may think they hate you now for what you do, but I promise you they will love you more later on for saving their lives.

It is especially painful to drive past a correctional institution on a Sunday morning or Sunday afternoon and observe the family reunions taking place. There are grandparents and parents, brothers and sisters all waiting to see loved ones who have been incarcerated for mistakes that have been made along the way. Many of these families have over time lost what little they owned paying lawyers to get their children out of jail time and time again, after having been promised by their children that they would never go back again. Families have been destroyed by eliminating pain in situations where pain was perhaps the only effective teacher. Love your children enough to allow them to feel pain. And remember, the sooner you do it the less it will cost you, your family, your children, and their family!

Here are a few tips to consider:

- **Begin teaching the lesson of accountability as soon as your child is able to understand and communicate.** Emphasize over and over again what you expect of your children, explain the consequences if they choose not to live up to those expectations, and then deliver on your promises. The first time a child senses inconsistency or that your standards or rules are without substance, you have lost. This does not mean you should create an environment where a child is afraid to relax or give them the impression that your role is to act as a drill sergeant. The idea is to have a code or standard of living for your family and make sure you live up to it.

- **Be consistent.** Over the years there has been a rule in our home that television is not allowed during the school year on a weekday with the exception of the national news. It was understood by our oldest child that this was the rule and he accepted it for the most part for many years. This continued without any problem until one day during one of my husband's extended business trips, in an effort to spend time with our son to try to make up for his father's absence, I allowed him a few hours of television during the week. After my husband returned home, my son thought, "Oh well, that rule about no television doesn't apply any longer because mom allowed me to change it." He turned on the television one evening and my husband wanted to know why the sudden change in obeying the rules, and asked that he turn it off. My son replied, "But mom let me." You can figure out the rest of the story. What is interesting, however, is that a rule that from the outset was accepted without any resistance had suddenly become a point of contention, because I presented the element of inconsistency.

- **Make your children responsible and accountable for their own space.** Following the purchase of our first home it became necessary to hire someone to help with the cleaning. We were going through the process of restoring our home and were doing most of the restoration ourselves. This meant that between our professional work, parenting, and working on the restoration, finding time to clean the house properly was next to impossible. Our son, who was around six or seven at the time, decided that he no longer needed to remove the dirty linen from his bed or pick up around his room because "we" had a cleaning lady. Well, I immediately corrected him to let him know that the cleaning lady was hired for his father's and my convenience and not his because we worked everyday. He thought this was the most ridiculous thing he had ever heard but we stuck by our rule that the cleaning lady was to clean every area of the house with the exception of his room. Our message to him was, if you sleep in the bed, then it is your responsibility to make it. As I write this, our son is in boot camp in the US Navy, so I trust his lesson is coming in handy!

Though this may seem like a minor lesson, teaching a child to be responsible for the space around them will in later years translate into other areas of being accountable for situations they create. Getting this message through to a child early in life will also help them understand that if a situation in which they find themselves is unacceptable, then it is their responsibility to do something about it. Many children grow into adults who are incessant whiners because they have learned at home that whining gets results.

- **Rules broken outside the home are no longer under the guidelines of expected consequences set up in your home.** It is important to teach children that rules and guidelines set up in society are designed to create a safe, just, and effective environment to serve the needs of society as a whole. They should be taught very early on that institutions created to enforce these rules do not necessarily have the time, flexibility, or disposition to permit individual excuses for violating these rules. Communicate to children very early on that if they understand the rules and guidelines and still decide not to abide by them, they will have to live with the consequences.

Perhaps one of the most popular phrases among young people is, "It isn't fair." A constant reminder should be given that life isn't fair nor was it designed to be. What is true is that rules and the punishment for not adhering to them were designed by society, and designed to serve society. This fact is the most important reason why children need to be brought up in an environment, at home, where there are standards and consistent guidelines. A child who is not given this foundation will be released into a world that will toss them about in ways in which they may never be able to recover. Remember, your lessons will be administered with love and understanding and the "pain" you cause for your child will be given in love and will nurture them. Prison systems, on the other hand, aren't designed to nurture.

- **Don't teach "It's not my fault."** Being overprotective is one of the greatest pitfalls of most otherwise effective parents. Because of a parent's role as protector and teacher, most will automatically accept the blame in situations involving their children, or try to deflect this blame elsewhere (as long as it is away from their child). It is important to analyze each situation and make certain that if a child has created a problem, he or she should accept responsibility. Taking the blame yourself or trying to shift the blame elsewhere only sends the message "I am not responsible for my actions."

chores:

_____

_____

_____

_____

_____

From the Good Earth

Talk to a child and you will inspire for a moment; show a child and you will influence for a lifetime. One of the most important things a parent can do for a child is to set an example to live by. Every act of living is an opportunity to teach a child a lesson and build a foundation that will be lasting and meaningful to the future of your family.

Many of the values and survival skills practiced by past generations deserve remembering and teaching. Today's children, as well as children of recent generations, are bombarded with information "telling" them what to do, but not a lot of reasons why or explanations how. It comes as no surprise, then, that children are confused and seeking answers in things that are detrimental to the overall purpose of what a family was meant to be.

Gardening is just one of the effective ways parents can teach valuable lessons to their children while at the same time instilling values and a sense of overall purpose. This chapter outlines six important lessons you can teach by planting a garden: responsibility, love, patience, giving, cooperation, and the reward of hard work.

RESPONSIBILITY

One of the greatest benefits of teaching a child how to garden is that the child learns how to be responsible. Gardening can be a lot of fun, but it is involves responsibility. Each phase of the gardening process requires a person to be diligent, caring and committed to the goal of having the garden be a success.

To begin the process of teaching the lesson of responsibility, it is important that in the beginning you share part of the responsibility. For example, you may want to share in the planting, and alternate responsibility for things like watering and weeding between yourself and your child. If there are multiple children in the family, it is a good idea to plant individual gardens of vegetables or flowers for which they will be responsible. This technique will allow them the opportunity to gauge their individual progress. You should consider combining their gardens in the future in order to teach them the lesson of teamwork and working together as a family unit.

After you have had an opportunity to work out the schedule for caring for your garden, allow your child the time to carry out his or her share of the responsibility on their own without your intervention. It is important that you not remind them more than a few times about what it is they are to do. It may mean that they will lose a part of their garden but the loss will impress upon them how important it is to take that responsibility seriously. Lessons such as these are what teach the concept of actions and consequences, and will make an impression far greater than any words you might be able to speak to them.

PATIENCE

One of the biggest problems facing our children today is the difficulty in learning and understanding the value of patience. Our present society is based on instant gratification and therefore creates in all of us the urge to do and have now! Unfortunately, one who lacks patience will typically lack an understanding of the value and reward of hard work, and of setting and accomplishing goals, as well as lack a basic appreciation for the critical elements in leading a meaningful and purposeful life.

To teach this lesson, begin by planning with your child a garden for the Spring or early Fall. You should allow him or her to help with the research and with making the decision of what to plant. Vegetables are always a nice choice for a child's garden, since they will not only they learn how to use their efforts to grow plants, but how to harvest, prepare, and eat them later in the year!

To get started, you may want to visit your local bookstore or library to get a comprehensive book on the subject. To have your child grasp a complete understanding, begin early enough in the season in order to allow the use of seeds. This will provide you with an opportunity to teach the importance of sowing seeds and relate this to important areas in their lives. For example, you can discuss with them what happens when small tasks are completed and how they multiply into greater things. You may also want to add a few starter plants which can be purchased at the local garden center. By using a combination of seeds and small plants you will be able to teach about the different stages of life. Be sure to keep the seed packets as markers to remind them of what their patience will reap once the wait is over. Laminating the seed packets and attaching them to a dowel rod using jute cord will help the seed packets withstand rain, wind and watering in the garden. A visit to the produce market to see examples of the kinds of vegetables being grown in their garden will also help your child become excited about their endeavor.

Instruct your child how the garden should be planted and have him or her share in the responsibility for its care. Set aside thirty minutes at least three times a week to spend with your child to work in the garden and check on its progress. It is also a good idea to allow your older children to spend some time alone to make their own discoveries, which could perhaps be used as a basis for discussion later on.

While spending time with your child in the garden, take time to talk about what is taking place as you wait for the first sprouts to appear. Be sure to relate this experience to things that are taking place in his or her life. Time spent in the garden can prove to be very valuable as there are fewer distractions and the quiet time provides an atmosphere to allow for a new level of bonding between the two of you.

LOVE

After planting the seeds, use this opportunity to draw an analogy of what happens when an expression of love is given. Explain to them that, like a seed, love begins to grow and multiplies until finally it spreads into every area of your life. Love is very much like planting seeds and should therefore be expressed whenever an opportunity is presented. Explain also that the opposite effect occurs when hateful acts are committed. As with love, these acts also spread and result in the tearing down rather than the building up of the good things around us. This stage of gardening can also be used to teach the importance of loving and caring for those things in our lives that are important. Explain that just as plants require love and caring in order to grow, parents have been placed in their lives to provide these things and assure that their children grow into strong and caring adults. This exercise will prove to be important for both you and your child because as you are teaching them, you will also be reminded to examine the quality of your efforts in providing for their needs.

GIVING

The lesson of giving can be taught at both the beginning and end of the gardening cycle. As you begin your garden, be sure to relate to your children that the more time and effort they put into caring for the garden, the better his or her chances become of experiencing success. Explain that like the daily care you provide for them — feeding, providing support, and weeding out situations that can be detrimental to their well-being — they too must adopt the same attitude toward caring for their garden. Feeding assures proper growth and the health of the plant; staking, as in the case of tomato plants, provides support to allow the plant to grow sturdy and strong; and weeding helps to protect the plants from harmful weeds which will ultimately destroy the plants if they are allowed to continue to grow. Explain that like stakes, a family is there to provide support when difficult situations arise until they are unable to stand on their own. It is important to teach them that it is okay to need the support of one's family, and they should be assured that their family will always be there during their time of need.

...like a seed, love begins to grow and multiply until it finally spreads into every area of your life...

Bonnie W. McDaniel

COOPERATION

As you are planning and after you begin working in the garden, explain to your child that this is an effort which requires the cooperation of all elements involved in helping the garden to grow. The plants require rain, sun and the care of each of you in order to live. Explain that the success of your garden is very much like what you as a parent require in order to raise children. It requires the cooperation of everyone, which includes parents, children, and community in order for the parenting process to work. Your child should be taught to understand that of everyone involved, his or her role and cooperation is the most important.

THE REWARD OF HARD WORK

As you progress through each stage of the growth of your garden, make sure to let your child know how proud you are of him or her. After you are able to begin harvesting from your garden, be sure to plan a special meal with your child where you can prepare some of the vegetables from his or her garden. If you have also included flowers in your garden, which I would recommend that you do, be sure to cut a few to dress up the table to make this occasion extra special. And remember to take lots of pictures!

Springtime is nature's way of letting us know that all is right with the world. This time of year really gets me excited with dreams of grand gardens; it also sends my husband packing because he knows the "dirt queen" has been released from Winter's prison once again.

I remember the first garden I planted after being married and the look of disbelief on my husband's face when I announced that the two-foot by four-foot piece of earth in front our town house would be ideal to grow tomatoes and zucchini. He knew he had married a small town girl, but "farming" as he called it was out of the question. You see, my husband spent his early childhood in the inner city, and although in later years his family built a lovely home in the suburbs, he believed that gardens were for flowers and vegetables were things you purchased at the local market.

And so, yours truly had some convincing to do. My son and I embarked on a mission of proving to my husband that we could plant a vegetable garden and the neighbors were not going to start a petition to pass zoning laws banning our little enterprise. The crop that year was a good one and even to this day, my husband is convinced that I bought the mammoth-sized zucchini produced on that little patch or earth. What my husband failed to realize is that I was more than just a good gardener. As a child, I discovered the secret to my contentment in my grandmother's garden. So often, when I need quiet time and answers to life's questions, I seek and find them in my garden. Many of the valuable lessons taught to me by my grandmother were taught as we talked and paid annual homage to the miracles found in the good earth.

There is something about planting a seed and watching it grow that is nothing short of a miracle — the kind of miracle that is perhaps needed in the lives of many our children. As I recall those days, what I have discovered is that, while at the time, I thought my grandmother was teaching me about gardening, she was really teaching me about life. I have tried over the years to teach my children pretty much the same things, using the vast wisdom of my grandmother. I know there have been pieces left out here and there, or maybe I have foolishly modified some of the lessons to give them my own twist. I also know, however, that in whatever form they have been passed on, something wonderful is certain to emerge.

My son is no longer a little boy, but has grown into a fine young man. It is interesting that he doesn't care for zucchini, and except for spaghetti sauce, doesn't like tomatoes either. And although it would have been nice to have his first garden influence his selection of things to eat, I realize that that really wasn't the point anyway.

As with Spring, each new phase of life offers an opportunity for life to begin anew. And if the seeds have been sown well, and given the proper food with loving hands and kind words, each of us can experience the wonderful miracles in store for each of our lives.

Make a commitment today — plant a garden and discover the miracles in store for your life and the lives of your children. And remember, no matter where you live, our world begins at home.

Bonnie W. McDaniel

With Our Own Hands

Many of the basic skills of everyday living which parents used to teach their children are no longer being taught, either by parents or in our schools. Arts and crafts — from painting and carpentry to sewing and pottery — are dying in popularity among younger generations because parents no longer see the need to teach these skills to their children, or in many instances, they themselves lack the skills and knowledge to pass on.

So much satisfaction is provided to a child when they learn how to plan and complete a project. It is important that we place a new emphasis on passing along this knowledge, if only as a means of preserving the rich artistic heritage we all share. If you can't personally teach these skills to your children because you lack the skills or knowledge, this can be easily remedied with the help of friends, family, extension courses at your local schools, and even the elderly at your local nursing home. Remember, our elderly look forward to being able to share their knowledge and wisdom — you need only ask.

The following are just a few of the benefits you will give your children and provide for your family simply by teaching them how to use their hands.

CREATIVITY

Have you ever noticed how everything in our world has its own unique thumbprint? Not one of God's creations is exactly the same. Human beings were also created with their own special ability to create and envision things uniquely and differently, never quite the same as the next person. It is through our own individual abilities to create and see things differently that we are provided individual meaning and purpose to our existence here on earth. To develop these individual abilities, however, it is important to provide our children with an environment where their creativity is nurtured.

As parents, many of us have a secret (or not so secret!) desire to see our children grow up to become doctors, lawyers, or great world leaders. As a result of our desire to raise "important" people, though, we sometimes fail to nurture the skills and interests our children may have been born to fulfill. It is important that you not use your children as vehicles to try live out your own unfulfilled dreams. This is especially true among contemporary women who discourage teaching their daughters things that would relegate them to being looked upon by modern society as "simply" homemakers. Remember, it is in good homes that we teach and nurture world famous leaders and Nobel peace prize winners and presidents, male and female. Therefore, homemakers and nurturing homes are not only important, they are vital.

BUSY HANDS ARE GREAT SPIRIT-SOOTHERS

Needlepoint is used frequently by hospitals as one of the most effective tools for treating depression. Working with one's hands has an amazing healing and calming effect on people by providing quiet time, an outlet when life becomes difficult to manage, and also the satisfaction of personal accomplishment. As parents, it is important to remember that it is a combination of all things — from passive entertainment to active work — which provide the balance our children need to lead meaningful and productive lives.

TEACH FISHING

"Give a man a fish and you feed him for a day. Teach a man how to fish and you feed him for a lifetime." So goes the economics of knowing how to work with your hands. And of course, this ancient Chinese proverb applies to women as well!

Nothing learned is ever wasted! Teaching your children how to care for themselves through the use of their creative talents will only serve to enhance their ability to lead successful lives. And who knows: what begins one day as just a hobby or an interest could very well end up as a job that helps pay for college, or a career that turns into them into a billionaire and/or a world famous artist!

BUSY HANDS BUILD CHARACTER

Character distinguishes individuals on many levels — by reputation, moral firmness, strength, and more. A person with notable character is hard to describe, but once you meet them you know who they are. In general, they are people who are clear about who they are and have worked very hard to determine what is meaningful and important in their lives. Perhaps they are humanitarians, or public servants, or volunteers, or business leaders; they are also your coworkers, neighbors, family, and friends. In every case, these people did not build character overnight. It comes by working, living, seeing, loving, caring, teaching, listening, and growing; it comes by experiencing life, which requires getting involved in life, and getting engaged in reality.

Busy hands help children grow because while working with their hands, their inner strength is "secretly" being nurtured (note to parents: don't tell your children this or they might not want to participate!). When I finally understood this, all of the lessons of learning how to work with my hands gained clarity, and I finally understood why my grandmother thought it was so important to teach me.

From House to Home

Many families have been destroyed because of their perceived need to "keep up with the Jones's." Their thinking is "the grander the structure and its collection of goods, the happier the family." Of course, this couldn't be farther from the truth. If you are able to comfortably afford a large home and decorate it with fine antiques and expensive art, and buy your children the latest stereo systems and cars, then it is your choice to do so. Do not, however, expect that accumulating all this wealth will bring your family the happiness you seek. Let the malls, museums, and offices preserve wealth; it's homes which preserve families.

Some of the nicest homes I have visited have been very simple in design with tasteful and sometimes modest furnishings. What struck me above all else was their focus on creating spaces where children can grow and family members can gather to share the things that are most important in life. For example, a living room the size of a small gymnasium decorated with thousands of dollars in fine furnishings looks nice, but does very little to encourage conversation and create a comfortable atmosphere for families to come together, which is why "living" rooms were created in the first place. Like many people, I also grew up in a home where there was at least one room that was off limits and for "company visits" only, all donned in plastic furniture protectors that stuck to your bottom each time you tried to sit. What is interesting, though, is that when company finally did come over they usually ended up sitting in the kitchen or in the TV room where they could feel more at home.

Focus your attention on creating a home where your family can grow and live comfortably. And if you are feeling the need to spend time with a few good antiques, consider visiting a museum instead.

HOME IS WHERE THE HEART IS

Your home is where you and your family will spend many years. This dwelling should be representative of a place that is thought of with fondness, and a place that no matter where you venture, you can't wait to return.

BEGIN WITH A PLAN

Begin with a written plan for what you would like your home to look like. Use this as your guide, going one step at a time. Before getting started, though, you may wish to consider hiring a professional interior decorator to consult with you for a few hours. Their fee could more than pay for itself with huge savings in the long run. Remember, the final decision is for you and your family to make; the consultant is only there to help guide you through the process. Also remember to trust your instincts when it comes to what your family needs and what makes you feel comfortable in your home.

Once developed, your plan could take anywhere from a few months to a few years to implement depending on the kinds of changes needed within your home. By completing a plan, you will avoid giving your home the appearance of having been decorated "helter-skelter." Your plan should be flexible, though, to accommodate a change of heart, style, or circumstances, or a growing family. You can anticipate some of these changes in your original planning, but don't be afraid to go back to square one and start your planning all over again if your original plan just won't work anymore.

DECORATING TO CREATE SPACES FOR PRACTICAL LIVING

Just like kids who get the toy they want on Christmas morning but completely forget about it by Christmas afternoon, very often we forget we even own many of the things we once thought we so desperately needed. This, too, is the central lesson for creating a happy home. Set up your home to meet the emotional and physical needs of your family, and don't get caught in the trap of trying to decorate and entertain to the standards set by retailers and designers, whose primary interest is in selling products, not promoting healthy families. Your children and family are worth a lot more than that. For most hard-working families, spending unnecessarily usually means sacrificing precious time to work extra hours to pay for spending, or digging the family into credit card debt for things your family could very easily live without. Don't trade your children's futures for things. What families need is more time, and fewer things!

Strive instead to decorate your home to achieve a pleasant environment, but let your overall goal be one of practicality. Here are a few tips:

- **Start by focusing your efforts on windows, walls and floors.** These comprise the bulk of the areas affected most by our visual perception. If you work to achieve good color, texture and quality in these areas, the rest of the room will easily fall into place. In decorating these areas, be sure to make your selections based on the makeup of your family. For example, heavy draperies are impractical in rooms where your children will spend a lot of their time. Opt for light and airy curtains instead that could be easily made as part of a family project. The choice will also create a space that is more comfortable for the family by providing a room that feels less formal and will therefore be more comfortable.

- **For good quality furniture and low prices, check out estate sales.** A lot of the furniture found at estate sales tends to be offered by older couples who are simplifying their lives in their latter years. In most instances it has been well cared for and is usually of better quality than furniture manufactured today. Don't be thrown by the styles or colors; focus instead on comfort and quality. An older piece can be easily updated by adding slipcovers or having the piece reupholstered using updated fabric designs. The idea is that you will usually spend a fraction of what you would normally spend for a newer piece at a retail establishment. Also, be sure to check out thrift stores and yard sales for possible good finds. Remember the less money you require to live, the more time you will have to spend with your family, living.

- **Simplicity equals economical.** In choosing colors and furnishings remember to keep it simple. If you have a flair for the unusual, confine it to things like pillows or throws. Hot pink walls might be the rave this year but what will it look like a year from now when the designers say blue is definitely in? Choose basic colors instead and designs for the focal points of your room (windows, walls and floors). Keeping up to date is easily achieved by changing pillow covers, tablecloths or furniture throws.

- **Create a home that says "Welcome, please come in."** Over the years people have often commented to me how comfortable they have felt in my home. This is in spite of the fact that some of the pieces of furniture in my home tend to be on the formal side given my interest in antiques. What has made them seem less formal however, is the choices of colors and the integration of things that make up who my family is. I have no set or defined way of decorating a room. The rule is basically, "Does it make my family feel comfortable?" Another rule is that if another family visits, will it become necessary to put up a "Do not enter" sign in any room in our home? And of course, as I said earlier, remember that the most important rule for a home is that it should be a place where every member of your family will love to come home to.

- **Plan your purchases.** Using your plan, decide the best time to make purchases for the more expensive items for your home. Large purchases should be planned and budgeted at the beginning of the year with the goal being to pay for those purchases with cash. Family projects for things such as painting or fixing up can be added to the family calendar and implemented together as a family throughout the year.

OUT BACK IN THE KITCHEN

A warm and inviting kitchen is the center, the heartbeat, of a nurturing home. If you want a good indication of the mood of most homes, pay a visit to their kitchen. This is perhaps one of the most ideal areas of the house to bring the family together to talk and work together as you prepare the family meal. And if you are fortunate enough to have an eat-in kitchen or a breakfast area in your kitchen, then this is even better.

Bonnie W. McDaniel

Have you ever noticed that most new homes are missing something? I am one of those people who seek out new housing developments and am usually the first to sign in the visitors log. Although I prefer older homes, I enjoy basking in the creativity and freshness of a newly decorated one.

My husband and I recently purchased our fourth home, a 60-year old English colonial. After owning two newer homes and a 50-year old home many years ago, we couldn't wait to take on the challenge of owning and restoring an older home once again.

In addition to believing that they just don't make homes like they used to, we also like the unassuming architectural design found in most older homes. A prime example of this is the kitchen in our present home. Although it is lacking the spaciousness and conveniences of our previous home, I find this one to be so much more special. In addition to the beautiful old metal cabinets and oak wood floors are three bright windows over the kitchen sink.

When I first saw this kitchen, I knew immediately we had found our new home. To someone who has never had the opportunity to build memories while looking out the kitchen window, your probably wouldn't understand. But for those of you who have ….

One of the inconveniences of owning this older home, however, is that we have been temporarily relegated to doing dishes the old-fashioned way — by hand. During one of our evenings of doing the dishes, I stopped for a moment and realized just how much time we had spent in the kitchen washing, drying and putting away dishes — together. Here we were without tour trusty dishwasher of old, but instead of thinking about and dreading the work of having to clean the kitchen, we were laughing and talking about the day that had just passed.

I recalled how while growing up, I spent countless hours in the kitchen with my grandmother, and later on with my mother, doing dishes as we talked about everything from making biscuits to politics. Kitchen windows and doing dishes together seem to encourage that sort of thing. My mother and grandmother would remind me to dry the back of the dishes real good, as they reassured me in the same breath that a problem I might have been having at school or with a friend would surely work itself out. Just having them tell me that everything would be okay seemed to make it so. Those times meant so much to helping to make me feel secure.

Later that evening after the dishes had been done and neatly put away, I thought about the recent conversation and the laughter and asked myself if perhaps my daughter and husband had enjoyed our time in the kitchen as much as I had. I also wondered if years from now when my daughter had her own kitchen and was perhaps washing dishes with her son or daughter, she would remember.

And as I turned out the last light to officially end my day, it occurred to me, of course she would remember, just as I had, because kitchen windows and doing dishes together encourages that sort of thing.

If you have an eat-in area in your kitchen, then you have the ideal area to congregate for breakfast, snacks, or meals, during those times when you would prefer not to eat in the dining room. Perhaps my favorite floor plan, though, is one with a country or family style kitchen. These types of kitchens are especially nice because in addition to eating and preparing meals, it also allows a nice place for the kids to sit and talk with a parent while dinner is being prepared. It is also very easy to prepare dinner and help with the homework simultaneously for those parents who are short on time.

In order to set up your kitchen as a place for the family to hang out, begin by first removing the television. In the past I used the television to entertain myself while preparing meals or working in the kitchen. What I discovered however, is that it was very difficult for me to talk to my family with the distraction of trying to watch my favorite show. If you find it necessary to have entertainment in the kitchen for those times when you might be alone, try using a radio as an alternative. Radios are also useful, when tuned to the right program, in providing topics to discuss on things such as current news events or other topics provided on many of the family-oriented radio talk shows. The radio should be used only during those times that are non-family times whenever possible.

Following are a few suggestions for setting up a family kitchen in which your family will be able to build fond memories as well as teach valuable lessons to your children for years to come.

- **The basics.** First, since the kitchen is an area where your family will congregate, you should make a special effort to create an environment that is conducive not only to preparing meals, but to teaching meal preparation skills and spending time together.

  Begin by taking an inventory of your kitchen equipment and how things are currently organized. Then, think of what you would ultimately like to have in your kitchen, and move little by little toward where you would like to be. If this means moving (or even getting rid of!) anything that is non-functional to make room for things that are, then do it. There are many ways to stock your kitchen that minimize stress on your wallet: check out your local want ads for used small appliances (very often you will run across items that are unused and still in the box, but at a fraction of their original cost), garage sales, and estate sales. Don't forget to also check your weekly newspaper circulars for end of the season sales as well as manufacturer's outlets. It is also a good idea to share with your friends and family what you are trying to accomplish as very often they are looking for ideas for gifts at Christmas or for other special occasions. People usually are more interested in giving something to someone that they know they either need or will enjoy.

During this process, remember to relate to your children that the importance of setting up this special place is to not only provide an efficient work area to prepare food, but more importantly to prepare a place where your family can come together at the end of the day.

- **Don't restrict yourself.** Look at your kitchen as an area which houses more than just kitchen things. Make a list of all of the things that are special to your family and consider including some of these in your kitchen/eating area. Instead of the usual artwork designed especially for kitchens, consider framing family photos and hanging them in the eating area. Pictures of your children at play or working with you around the house are best. Save portrait-type photos for other areas of your home. Samples of art projects are also wonderful items to include on an art board created specifically to hang children's artwork. The idea is make this area as comfortable and inviting as possible to encourage your family to want to spend time there.

When deciding where to put different items, remember to take into consideration the makeup of your family. Organize your kitchen and eating area to allow for the involvement of the entire family. For example, if you are trying to teach a younger child to be responsible for setting the table, it is a good idea to place things like napkins, placemats, flatware, dishes and glasses in an area that is accessible to them. If the child is too young to handle breakable items you may want to keep these items up out of their reach and leave the other items for them to handle. Organizing them in lower drawers is a good way to allow them to be completely responsible without needing the assistance of an adult or older sibling.

Remember, this is a project which should include the entire family. Get input in the planning, and depending on your available space, allow each family member to contribute something that is representative of who they are. Ask questions and talk to your children as you plan with them and begin their lessons of why the family kitchen is important. This is also a great time to share some of your experiences as a child along with some of the lessons you might have learned and how they affected your life. If you are without any fond memories, explain to your children your desire to start to build fond memories, beginning with them.

- **Spending time.** Look at the color and lighting in your kitchen area and ask yourself and other members of your family if it is a place they would enjoy spending time. Colors affect a person's moods, so be extra careful to make sure you create an atmosphere that is both welcoming and conducive to people wanting to spend their time there. If you choose to change the color of your kitchen, be sure to consult with your children and spouse first. Remember, the goal is to create a family kitchen. There are a number of options available to creating just the right atmosphere including wallpaper, paint, textured walls, faux walls or any combination of these. If you have the resources, you may want to consider going even further by expanding the kitchen window, adding a patio off of the kitchen, knocking down a wall which separates your kitchen from your dining room, and more!

The Cycle of Life

Up to this point we have talked about home and raising children in the home — in the eye of the storm. Outside the walls of the home and even inside, though, moves the cycle of life — birth, growth, love and marriage, children and more growth, more of life, and in time, eventually death. Children need to understand this cycle to become complete human beings, and to fully appreciate their place in the world.

BIRTH

The idea of a person being given the privilege of becoming a vehicle through which a new life will emerge is difficult for the human mind to comprehend. It is perhaps one of the most significant contributions any human being will ever make during their lifetime. Yet, the physical act of having a child requires no previous experience, nor does one have to be certified or qualified to become a parent. In spite of the importance of this role however, most of us are given an equal opportunity, no matter what our backgrounds or previous experiences. Along with this privilege, parents are also given the power to define our world, regardless of the amount of effort they decide to put into it, by the simple fact that they are able to give birth. All of this responsibility makes parents the most important people on our planet. They must not take lightly the act of bringing forth a new life, nor should they act as though the act of bringing forth life has made them parents (except in the biological sense).

Birth is a time
to celebrate!

Birth, though, in spite of all these weighty and important asides, is time to celebrate, to stop and take notice because a new cycle is about to begin its course. Prepare yourselves, prepare your family, and prepare your home. Then prepare some more! Your local library or bookstore has access to hundreds of titles on how to do this — how to prepare the home and other children for the arrival of new babies, how to make the home more comfortable for them, and how to help them begin growing. Take time do your research, and remember to also ask parents, grandparents, and others in your circle of friends and family for advice, even after you've become an experienced parent; your learning should never stop. Through it all, don't forget to cherish and share the moments. Hectic as they will be — even with the best preparation — the growth and arrival of children to this world are memories you will hold very dear throughout the rest of your lives.

GROWTH

Most of what we have discussed to this point involves the growth of children and families. What hasn't been covered in much detail is the growth of parents. In order to become effective parents, there needs to be a clearly defined difference between who is the parent and who is the child, which means that once they become parents, adults need to assume their roles and responsibilities as such.

One important aspect of this distinction is that parents should not compete with their children. I'm not talking about sports or board games, but unhealthy competition for attention, which, as was mentioned earlier in the chapter on communication, often manifests itself as parents bickering with children on the level of children.

Another important aspect of this distinction is that parents must provide examples and guidelines to which children can aspire. A child cannot grow by looking at him or herself. In order for girls to know how to become grown women, it is imperative that they be given the opportunity to learn from and observe what women are supposed to be. It is preferable that this example be provided by their mother or a responsible female role model in the home. It is also a given that in order for boys to know and understand what it means to be a man, there must be an example of what a man should be and this should be provided through a process of nurturing and the setting of examples — once again, through a father or a responsible male figure, preferably at home.

By establishing a foundation and defining a code of conduct conducive to promoting healthy behavior for young women and young men, we can begin to foster the kinds of relationships that can lead to the creation of homes and families that epitomize what love and marriage are supposed to be.

LOVE AND MARRIAGE

Every human longs to be loved, but surprisingly and unfortunately, not all of us express our love consistently or in ways our children respond to. Saying "I love you" but coming home late from work everyday or always missing PTA meetings and school events is a wasted effort and makes children callous after a time. Show love by your actions as well as your words. Do things with your children, spend time with them, listen to them, help them grow, and grow with them.

Eventually, children will seek out relationships which mimic the ones they learned at home. This can be a good thing if the relationships in the home are good. It can also be bad if the relationships are dysfunctional or abusive. One sidenote that should be discussed along these lines is teen pregnancy. Many young girls talk about how nice it would be to have a baby, with the idea that babies are cute and that having one would give them something of their own to love. Many also see babies as a way of gaining attention from a boyfriend or a parent. Too often also, girls see the act of becoming a parent as a means of becoming an adult — of gaining control over their lives and ending painful situations in which they find themselves at home. Boys who are the fathers of these children are — just as with the girls — seeking ways to gain control over lives that are equally as painful and use this as a way of making a statement of their independence and becoming a man.

The phenomenon of love occurs when two like or compatible spirits meet and journey together to a destiny of one. Love is not physical, although very often it is the physical nature that attracts one human being to another. It is also not based on selection by profession or economics, although many people tend to think so.

Recently, I had the wonderful opportunity to spend a weekend with a group of teens who had been brought together to discuss and learn about this mysterious thing called love. It was a time for sharing as well as a time of trying to understand where and how the misconceptions concerning love are generated.

I walked away with an impression of one thing that seemed to be overriding in most of the conversations that occurred. Most of the young people at this event all agreed that their concept of love was derived through images. Those images are generated through the media, their peers, or watching their parents and others around them.

As a child I also saw many examples or images of love, most of them positive. But there were also those that were not so positive. Of all the images of love I experienced while growing up, one in particular remained pervasive in my mind as I looked forward to my first experience of falling in love. Down the block from my house lived a sweet couple whom we affectionately called Miss Mattie and Mr. Alex. The neighborhood children grew up watching as this couple, who — although they had been married for many years — courted and remained faithful to the special times set aside to share in their wonderful gift of love.

Over the years, I have continued to reflect on the beautiful image of this couple dancing on their big front porch, each time I hear Ray Charles singing "I Can't Stop Loving You." Although my experience of seeing this couple was one of a physical nature, I knew it was more than what it appeared.

As I watched them week after week, I could almost feel the melding together of their spirits as they danced in perfect

oneness, never speaking, yet knowing what the other was thinking. The smile on her face and the anticipation of waiting each Friday evening went far beyond any lyrics to a song or the smell of a familiar fragrance that served only as stimulation for the senses.

And when Alex stepped onto the porch and the two embraced, I knew this was love in its truest form. Their bond was special, and as a young girl, I knew it was something I, too, someday desired to have.

Mattie and Alex are long since deceased, but I often wonder if they knew what a wonderful impression they made on the neighborhood children by simply loving each other.

I found the other half of my special spirit and have been married to him for twenty-six years. We often dance around our living room floor as our daughter blushes to see her parents carry on like a couple kids in love. It is comforting to know that she and our son will not settle for anything less when it comes time to choose that special person with whom they will spend the rest of their lives. They, too, will wait for that special person, and like fitting together the pieces of a very intricate puzzle, know when the picture is complete.

And like Mattie and Alex and their mom and dad, they will spend their lives understanding and knowing that the real truth is found in waiting for love.

Bonnie W. McDaniel

If your teen is at risk — and even if they are not — here are a few things that each parent can do to try to help turn the tide:

- **Fill the void.** Remember that children are emotional vacuums in constant need of being filled. As a parent, it is important that you fill that void with things that are positive and worthwhile. Make a concerted effort to identify something they are good at or have a particular interest in and find ways to make this the focus every opportunity they are given. This is not something you can do hit or miss; it requires a consistent effort on your part.

- **Teach your sons to exercise responsible behavior.** Too often in focusing on the problems of teen pregnancy we focus on girls and their actions. This is not something that can take place without the willing participation of boys, too. Boys should be taught that this is not a situation that if created, they will be allowed to walk away from without any repercussions.

- **Pay attention to your children.** It is popular among most people to believe and accept the notion that sex education will solve this issue of teen pregnancy. What I have observed is that most children who are falling victims to this tragedy know precisely what it is they are doing and are choosing to take this path. Sex education, though important, should not be used as a substitute to satisfy the emotional needs of children.

Take the time to talk to them about everything. If you notice an increased interest in certain types of behavior, discuss it, don't avoid it. More importantly, try to determine what you might do to help them find, through positive behavior or activities, the things they feel they are needing. It is important, too, that you do not become a security guard in order to gain control over a situation that is perhaps already out of control. Let your children know that you want to trust them and that there is nothing more important to you than your love and concern for them. Remember also that if you desire to convince them of your sincerity, you must follow through on your words with actions.

Death, like birth, is an occasion we each have to experience. But also like birth, death is an occasion which should be celebrated, not so much as the ending of one's life, but as a celebration of all the things that happened over the course of a person's lifetime.

My grandmother died the year I turned nine years old. For the next thirty-three years, I found it difficult to remember very much about that day except for the pain of not having her in my life any longer. Then one Christmas, my aunt spoke to me about that day. As she related what happened, the memory of everything came back to me like rushing water, and though it brought me to tears, they were tears of joy because I discovered that my grandmother continued to live through the things she had taught those around her. Her life continued, because she had given all that had been given her to those who were left behind.

Many of us view death as the final stage where everything about a person ceases to exist. Death can also be seen, though, as a season where life as we know it moves from the planting to the bearing of fruit in the things we leave behind. Children can be taught to celebrate death if they are given the opportunity to grasp the richness of life in each moment, and understand how life continues after death in the things we remember, do, and pass onto others.

It is important to begin teaching this in the early stages of a child's life in order that it might become a part of who they are. Remind them of their heritage and things that were passed down through the years by those who came before; talk to your children about their similarities to other family members — the color of their eyes, the shape of their body, the sharpness of their mind, and other traits that are part of who they are; share the things that were taught to you by your mother, grandmother, grandfather, aunt, or uncle, and let them know how much you value these gifts and your understanding of the importance of passing them. By passing along our heritage in this manner, it helps instill in children a sense of responsibility for taking care of what is given to them. Encourage them to understand that in order to pass along memories and lessons to the next generation, it is important that they learn and care for these things.

When a loved one passes on, spend the time with your children, then, to talk about the legacy of the person. Be specific about what those things are and impress upon them the importance of taking seriously the significance of that person's life and its value to theirs.

It Matters

Each time a child learns to enjoy life, it matters. Each time a child learns how to be responsible, it matters. Each time we show a child love and affection, it matters. Each time we do things with children and teach by example, it matters. Each time we lift a child who has fallen and encourage them to continue on their way, it matters. Each time one child helps another, it matters. Each time one family reaches back to help another family, it matters.

The role of families in our society is critical. Yet it is easy to lose our way. We receive advice from every corner on how families should be raised, and indeed, our own nature as human beings causes us to want to choose our own way. But much wisdom and experience came before us, and we can find simple lessons in our past for how to improve our lives today.

Like a favorite recipe, families need just the right amount of the ingredients to make things come out just right. The good news is that these ingredients are available in every home — patience, responsibility, cooperation, love — and that adding them to a mix of activity and involvement will lead to family and individual lives filled with meaning and purpose.

Each new day presents an opportunity to improve our sometimes turbulent world with the things we say, do, and teach to our children. Seize the moment, take control of your destiny, and make your home the loving and nurturing place you and your children deserve — the calm in the eye of the storm.

Deigratia (by the Grace of God),

The Beginning...